Programming

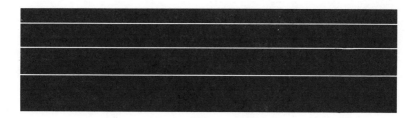

For Employee Services and Recreation

James A. Busser
University of Nevada, Las Vegas

Champaign, Illinois 61824-0673

This book is one in a series on Employee Associations produced by Sagamore Publishing in cooperation with the National Employee Services and Recreation Association. Other books in the series include: **Operating Employee Associations: Providing Employee Services and Recreation Programs,** and **Working With Volunteers in Employee Services and Recreation.**

©1990 Sagamore Publishing, Inc.

Printed in the United States of America

ISBN: 0-915611-29-5
Library of Congress Catalog Card Number: 90-62971

This book is dedicated to my wife, Cynny.

 ## *Acknowledgments*

Several National Employee Services and Recreation Association (NESRA) members assisted in facilitating the completion of this text by providing me with on-site tours and documents and by sharing their wealth of programming knowledge. These individuals include Phyllis Smith, Hughes Fullerton Employees Association; Bob Pindroh, Lockheed Employees Recreation Club; and Maxine Haun and Dan Kempken at Rockwell International. In addition, NESRA Book Committee members, specifically Betty Atchison, Pete DeFranco, Joe Haughlie and Patrick Stinson, reviewed the manuscript and provided suggestions for revisions.

NESRA members throughout the country contributed to this work by providing valuable information regarding the programs offered at their worksites. These individuals included Sue Potter, Nationwide Insurance Activities Association; Frank Deluca, Textron Lycoming; Peter DeFranco, Xerox Corporation; David Weiss, Cummins Employees Recreation Association; David DeVine, Chemical Abstracts Service; Debbie Patton, J C Penney Insurance; David J. Stapf, Ashland Petroleum Company; Randy Schools, National Institutes of Health, Robert Pfahler, Battelle — Columbus; Janiet Daniels, Columbia Gas Distribution Companies, Connie Fredkove, 3M club of St. Paul, Incorporated and Mark Ward, San Diego Gas and Electric Employees Association.

Several individuals from UNLV facilitated the accomplishment of this work. John Massengale allowed me the flexibility to spend time writing at home. Jerry Landwer provided relevant resources for the book and suggested revisions to parts of the manuscript. Randy Hale creatively developed the graphic illustrations. Mauri Collins reviewed the entire manuscript and provided insightful comments that improved the clarity of my writing.

Finally, Joseph and Peter Bannon provided their support and their Sagamore publishing staff meticulously nurtured the manuscript through to its final completion.

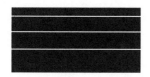 *Foreword*

NESRA proudly presents the newest publication in our employee services series, *Programming for Employee Services and Recreation*. Programming for a diverse workforce can be quite challenging for the emoployee services manager. This book answers such pertinent questions as how to assess employees' needs, the programs one should offer, and how to evaluate the programs' effectiveness.

An employee services program should reach the highest percentage of employees possible to make it beneficial to the organization. The changing demographics of today's and tomorrow's workforce will dictate what programs should be offered. There are obvious demographics that can be evaluated, such as sex and age. However, many more factors should be investigated. This book is a valuable resource in determining your employees' needs.

On behalf of NESRA, I wish to thank the research committee chaired by vice president Sue Potter, CESRA, of Nationwide Insurance Company; the book review committee consisting of Jim Alexander, CESRA, of PHIL/AERS; Betty Atchison-Bair, CESRA, of R.R. Donnelley & Sons Company; Pete DeFranco, CESRA, of Xerox Corporation; Joe Hauglie of Control Data Corporation; Phyllis Smith, CESRA, of Hughes Aircraft Company; the NESRA Board of Directors, and the NESRA Education and Research Foundation.

Patrick B. Stinson
NESRA Executive Director
September, 1990

v

Contents

ix

1

Introduction

Industrial recreation programs have grown from modest beginnings. A company opened a library for community use; other businesses provided sports programs for their employees; some organizations planned picnics and furnished their employees with clubhouses. It was from these roots that the first employee association was formed. Much has changed in the workplace since the inception of what are now referred to as employee services and recreation programs. Their contribution to the corporation and the employee continues to remain vital to the needs of both (Tober, 1988).

Employee services and recreation programs are now characterized by their eminent variety. Awarding a gold pin with the corporate logo signifying 25 years of employment, conducting lunch time exercise programs or art classes, facilitating the computer club's meeting, purchasing Christmas cards, promoting health, and providing a film processing service are all examples within the range of possible programs. These are a diverse set of activities whose common bond is the setting in which they take place.

These activities are representative of the unique role of employee services and recreation. At the core of this role is the actual involvement of employees in programs and services that meet their needs and fulfill management and employee expectations. The provision of programs and services that will be enjoyed by employees is perhaps the most challenging, and yet rewarding, aspect in the management of corporate employee services.

The goal of this book is to serve as a basis for developing and implementing programs and services that will satisfy employees. The book is not intended to be a comprehensive guide to program planning, but one that will provide an orientation to the program planning process, address some issues pertinent to the corporate setting, and act as a reference that will stimulate the pursuit of further information. It is hoped that this book will be a useful contribution to all managers and volunteers involved in the provision of employee services and recreation programs.

The Program Planning Process

The planning of employee services and recreation programs is a future-oriented process that reduces uncertainty and chance. Program planning is a continuous process that requires diligent efforts and careful attention. Planning is a goal-oriented process that is intended to determine and address the benefits to be derived by the company and the employee as a result of the provision of and involvement in employee services and recreation programs. It is important not only to identify the goals to be achieved through the provision of services, but also to articulate the means to achieve them (York, 1982). This is the underlying role of the manager who is responsible for employee services and recreation programs.

The program planning process, outlined in Figure 1.1, is only briefly discussed in this chapter. Expanded discussion of this model will continue throughout the remainder of the book. In addition to the program planning process, brief descriptions of actual employee services and recreation programs are provided. It is hoped that these will stimulate the consideration of new services and programs for inclusion in currently existing programs or encourage the start of an employee services and recreation department.

Mission of Employee Services and Recreation

Figure 1.1 suggests that the mission of the employee services and recreation department or association should provide direction throughout the development, provision, and evaluation of employee services and recreation programs. An appropriate mission is based on the potential benefits that may be realized to the corporation and employees as a result of

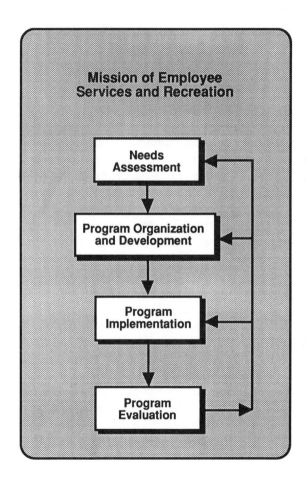

Figure 1.1

voluntary employee participation in recreation programs and services. Gaining an understanding of potential benefits is at the center of developing this philosophical perspective, which in turn provides a foundation for the goals of the association and identifies the scope of program offerings. Determining the mission of employee services and recreation is a vital component of the planning process.

Needs Assessment

A needs assessment is a key component of the program planning process because it provides employees with the opportunity to identify the programs and services they feel will address their particular needs and interests. A needs assessment becomes a research tool that provides the corporation with a basis for developing programs and services from the perspective of the identified needs and interests of employees. It can be characterized as generating program ideas through the involvement of employees while also developing the employees' relationship with the program that nurtures their continued participation.

Program Organization and Development

In this phase of the program planning process, the goals and objectives for the program are developed. Articulated goals and objectives provide a direction for the development of the program while also serving as a useful reference in the evaluation process. Goals are statements that specify the intent of the program. Objectives are specific behavioral outcomes that program participants are expected to acquire as a result of their involvement. In this stage of the program planning process, the program formats also are chosen. Formats are structures that are determined to be the best method of facilitating the goals and objectives of the program. Such formats include clubs, tournaments, competitions, special events, and seminars.

Program Implementation

At this stage of the program planning process, the event has been developed and now the program is to be implemented. There are many tasks to be accomplished at this stage. However, our discussion focuses on a few that are more relevant. Contracting for programs, pricing, and services are among the important implementation functions of the employee services manager. In addition, advertising and promoting the program, corporate liability, and worker's compensation will be examined.

Program Evaluation

Program evaluation is an important aspect of the programming process. Evaluation is a procedure that is used to determine the worth of the program or service to the corporation, association, and employees. A mechanism should be in place that takes the information obtained through evaluation and feeds it back into the programming process. There are several types of program evaluations that can be employed. Three types of evaluations particularly relevant to employee service and recreation will be discussed in this book: process, participant satisfaction, and efficiency.

Scope of the Book

This chapter has sought to introduce the role of program planning as a core ingredient in the coordination of an employee services and recreation program. Chapter 2 will explore the corporate philosophy and the benefits and mission of employee services and recreation programs. Chapter 3 will examine the methods of conducting a needs assessment and the type of information that may be collected from employees. In Chapter 4, the organization and development of programs and services are discussed. Descriptions of various employee services appear in Chapter 5, and programs are discussed in Chapter 6. Chapter 7 addresses some pertinent issues in the implementation of services and programs, and Chapter 8 highlights evaluation procedures. Finally, Chapter 9 addresses factors affecting the future of corporations and resulting implications for the provision of employee services and recreation programs.

References

Tober, P. (1988). Historical perspective: The evolution of employee services and recreation. *Employee Services Management*, 31(1), 11-16.

York, R. O. (1982). *Human service planning*. Chapel Hill, NC: The University of North Carolina Press.

2

Mission of Employee Services and Recreation

The provision of employee services and recreation programs encompasses the efforts made by the corporation and the employee association to improve the quality of worklife for all employees. Quality of worklife is defined as "a process by which all members of the organization, through appropriate and open channels of communication, have some say in decisions that affect their jobs in particular, and the work environment in general, resulting in greater satisfaction and reduced levels of stress" (Schuler, 1987; p. 437). Quality of worklife is a phrase that represents a philosophical orientation in the workplace that is often referred to as organizational culture, or management style, through which employees experience feelings of ownership, self-control, responsibility, and self-respect.

It is the organizational environment that is the primary focus for programming designed to enhance the quality of worklife through employee services and recreation programs. Improving the quality of worklife refers to activities that impact the conditions that affect an employee's experience at the workplace. Some of the quality of worklife activities relevant to employee associations include providing opportunities for (1) individual choice, (2) participation in decisions, (3) safety and health, (4) development of human resources, and (5) satisfaction of social needs (Hellriegel, Slocum & Woodman, 1989). The provision of these activities by the corporation focuses on improving employee satisfaction, increasing job involvement and productivity, and reducing stress, turnover, and absenteeism while enhancing profits, competitiveness, and survival for the organization (Schuler, 1987).

The mission of an employee association stems from this quality of worklife perspective and provides guidance in the determination and provision of employee services and recreation programs. Further, this philosophical perspective suggests the distinct contribution that employee services and recreation programs offer to the employee and the corporation. Employee associations are in a unique situation. Their mission must be a blending of the values of all the corporate actors involved, including management, the employees, and the professional association staff.

The mission of employee services and recreation drives the development of specific goals that focus on and impact the range of programs and services provided to employees. In addition, each phase of the program planning process is affected by this mission. Employee associations can provide a wide array of employee services and recreation programs. To articulate the mission that underlies the provision of services and programs requires an examination of both the issues and the benefits that accrue to the corporation and the employees from participating in an organized program.

Issues and Benefits of Employee Services and Recreation Programs

There are many benefits to the corporation that are attributed to employee participation in recreation programs and services. Most common are the improvement of employee morale and productivity, development of a feeling of unity within the company, improvement of the company's public image by showing a genuine concern for its employees' welfare, establishment of more open lines of communication within the company, development of rapport between different levels of employees and management, and the valuation of employees through recognition and appreciation (Debats, 1981). There is support for some of these benefits.

One of these potential benefits, employee morale, was a term instituted by personnel specialists and social psychologists that encompassed the often vague attitudes that employees hold regarding their work. Job satisfaction has replaced employee morale as a more definable and measurable variable. Job satisfaction is an attitude that depends on an evaluation made by employees of their jobs and surrounding organizational environments. This evaluation is comprised of two components: (1) what the employee actually experiences at work, and (2) the values and the desire for rewards the employee brings to the workplace (Heneman, Schwab, Fossum & Dyer, 1986). A high correspondence between the two components results in a high level of job satisfaction. However, when the desire for rewards does not match the actual experience, dissatisfaction results.

Many researchers have investigated the importance of job satisfaction, and their research studies indicate that employees with low job satisfaction are more likely to be absent from work. Further, job satisfaction is considered to be one of the major factors influencing the choice of whether to leave an organization or remain. Job satisfaction, then, is a predictor of job turnover (Baron, 1983).

Shinew and Crossley (1989) investigated the absenteeism rates and the job satisfaction of 900 employees at the General Electric Company. These employees were subdivided according to their involvement in company-sponsored recreation and fitness activities. The categories of employees included (1) members of GE's fitness center, (2) members of the GE Employee Activity Association, (3) members of both the fitness center and association, and (4) non-members. Significant differences in job satisfaction and absenteeism were found between members and non-members, but there were no differences between fitness center members and association members. Specifically, employees who were members of either the fitness center or the association were absent less often from their work than non-members. Similarly, fitness center and association members had higher levels of job satisfaction than non-members. The results of this study are consistent with other findings indicating the potential benefits in terms of employee satisfaction and lower absenteeism to be gained from employee participation in fitness and recreation programs.

In another study, Finney (1985) found support for the premise that participation in employee services and recreation programs contributes to higher employee productivity. In addition, this study, conducted at the Lockheed Employee Recreation Center, indicated that corporate provision of opportunities for recreation participation provides employees a perception of personal control, which may be lacking in their jobs. Voluntary participation in recreation programs allows employees to have the perception of control and, as a result, reduces employees' stress levels.

Issues and Benefits of
Wellness Services and Programs

A financial concern for organizations is the high cost of the health insurance that is provided to employees as a fringe benefit. Health care costs are increasing by 12 to 15 percent each year (Everly, 1985). Schott (1984) stated that "health care stands out as the single most inflationary factor in the American economy today" (p. 25). While there are a variety of factors that have impacted upon health care costs, the financial burden has been passed on to the consumer, specifically the employer. Health Maintenance Organizations (HMOs) represent one attempt to combat the rising costs of health care. HMOs have become prolific as organizations have seized this opportunity to offset increasing health care costs.

In addition to health care costs, organizations also have been increasingly concerned with the effects of occupational stress. The consequences of prolonged exposure to stress have been shown to be related to coronary heart disease, peptic ulcers, depression, alcohol and substance abuse, and increased cigarette smoking (Beehr and Newman, 1978). The health of employees directly affects the health care costs absorbed by the corporation.

The effects of stress have also impacted the organization in other ways. An organization's effectiveness can be seriously jeopardized by the occupational stress affecting its employees. High levels of stress have been shown to reduce both the quantity and quality of work produced. Additionally, employees under high levels of stress are more likely to be dissatisfied with their jobs (Steers & Rhodes, 1978), which leads to absenteeism and turnover (McKenna, Oritt & Wolf, 1981). Voluntary turnover is a significant financial burden for an organization. Other associated stress effects include increased conflict in the workplace and a rise in the number of grievances, accidents, strikes, and cases of sabotage and the incidence of employee burnout (Schuler, 1980). Kahn (1981) discovered that a decrease in the quality of working relations occurs under high levels of occupational stress, where work relations were marked by distrust, disrespect, and animosity. Seyle (1974) suggested that individuals may experience a loss of vitality from stress, resulting in lowered morale, motivation, and satisfaction. Employee stress may also impair an organization's effectiveness through communication breakdowns, faulty decision making, and lost opportunities (Quick & Quick, 1984).

In a proactive attempt to address issues related to health care costs, organizations have turned to health promotion in the form of employee fitness, health, and wellness programs. Approximately 50,000 U. S. organizations are involved in worksite health promotion (Ardell, 1985). On-site fully equipped fitness centers are provided by some 1,000 companies (Trenk, 1989). It is also estimated that more than 1,000 organizations spend over two billion dollars annually on health promotion. Wellness programs have become a major component of corporate health promotion as indicated by the more than 5,000 organizations that provide formal wellness programs (Cunningham, 1982). The overriding reason for corporate enthusiasm for wellness programs is the belief in cost containment (Ardell, 1985). In fact, "health care economists agree that wellness programs are perhaps the most effective and definitely the best long-range weapon we have to combat rising health care costs" (Hayes, 1986).

Wellness is a relatively recent concept that received increased attention during the 1970s. Stimulating the interest in the wellness concept was increasing dissatisfaction with traditional models of health. Everly (1985) described a continuum of health from traditional models, which focus on illness, to a wellness orientation. This continuum has several important aspects, the first being that the absence of illness is its center point in the model. Wellness is considered to be more than just the absence of disease. The wellness concept emphasizes the presence of positive emotional, mental, and spiritual states. Second, wellness is affected by the beliefs and behaviors under control of the individual. Therefore, changing one's lifestyle can contribute to increased levels of health.

Further support for a wellness model of health was provided by the data that suggest that it is our lifestyle that has a significant effect on the length of our lives and the level of our health (Laughlin, 1982). Everly (1985) reported that lifestyle accounts for 51% of all diseases. Several studies have shown that lifestyle behaviors such as smoking, dietary preferences, and the abuse of alcohol play a major role in mortality and morbidity (Miller, 1983).

In fact, the major causes of death for adults include heart disease, cancer, and strokes (Sloan, Gruman & Allegrante, 1987). Responding to the increased influence of lifestyle on health, the 1980 Surgeon General's Report of Health Promotion and Disease set out specific, measurable objectives for reducing those behaviors that increase the risks associated with disease and mortality. Five of these objectives are directly related to health promotion. These include smoking cessation, improved nutrition, exercise and fitness, stress control, and the reduction of drugs and alcohol. Wellness proponents suggest that reducing the level of these unhealthy behaviors should limit the incidence of diseases associated with lifestyle (Grossman, 1981). The fostering of a wellness lifestyle, then, could result in the prevention of these diseases (Townes, 1984).

The proposed benefits of wellness programs are broad and include such factors as increased employee satisfaction and productivity, reduced absenteeism, and reduced health care costs. These benefits are increasingly being measured, and research studies are appearing that offer some support for the value of these programs. One recent four-year study of 15,000 Control Data Corporation employees found a link between unhealthy employee behavior and health insurance premiums. The major finding of this research was that employees with the poorest lifestyle habits also had the highest medical claims. Several similar studies are presently under way that will compare death and illness data to several lifestyle behaviors (James, 1987).

Reasons for Employee Involvement

While employees participate in services and programs for some of the same reasons as previously stated, there are additional factors to consider. Employees at 16 organizations that belong to the National Employee Services and Recreation Association across the U. S. responded to a survey of the reasons for their participation in their employee association programs.

The employees identified social benefits, improved physical fitness, personal growth, competition, savings, and convenience as major factors influencing their involvement in programs and services. Additionally, employees indicated that participation in recreation programs and services offered them the opportunity to reduce their stress and pressure levels, increase their morale while also improving their skills, stimulate creativity, and open up new doors (Streitz, 1986). The employees' reasons for participation are equally important to consider in the development of a mission and goals to meet employee and corporate desires.

Management and Employee Support

Management support of employee services and recreation departments is a key ingredient in the complete functioning of these units. There is no question that gaining management support is a critical factor in the potential success of an employee services and recreation department. Management support provides the direction or goals for the department and ensures that employee services and recreation programs remain a valuable and stable component of the benefits provided by an organization.

The development of an employee service or recreation program designed to meet the specific needs of employees and enhance the potential benefits to the company, along with a clear statement of the goals and objectives to be accomplished, will foster support from management. Such programs should be supported through documented, quantifiable outcomes that provide feedback to managers on the progress of the program. Presentation of these results to managers, along with the relevant literature, will go far to document the importance of employee services and recreation programs and gain management support.

One dilemma often faced by employee associations and employee services and recreation departments is a lack of direction and support from top management. Gaining management support requires an understanding of the recent research and literature regarding the documented benefits of participation in em-

deterred from developing a philosophical base and articulating specific goals for the services and programs they provide. In the long run, a well-conceptualized and well-implemented program may gain crucial support when results are recorded through program evaluation.

When management does support employee services and recreation programs, this should be clearly demonstrated to employees. Associations can actively solicit visible management involvement. Managers may demonstrate their support through letters and memos to employees, interviews highlighting the importance of employee services, role modeling by participation in events, disseminating information at staff meetings, and other endorsements. Ideally, management could foster a corporate culture that values participation in employee services and recreation programs.

It is also important to nurture the involvement and support of employees. This is certainly accomplished by providing programs and services that are responsive to employee needs. However, involving employees in association activities creates a sense of ownership and fosters their personal commitment. Employees who participate in programs and services, who serve as volunteers or leaders, are, in essence, intertwined with association activities and have a stake in contributing to its success. Employees can also contribute by utilizing their particular occupational skills in the development of materials, by analyzing data, or by serving on relevant committees (Cataldo, Green, Herd, Parkinson, & Goldbeck, 1988).

Summary

The mission guiding the provision of employee services and recreation programs should reflect the purpose and benefits desired by the association, the company, and the employees. A mission provides direction to the association and assists in each phase of the program planning process. It is important to understand the perspectives of employees, corporation, association staff, and management in order to effectively develop and implement employee programs and services.

References

Ardell, D. B. (1985). *The history and future of wellness.* Dubuque, IA: Kendall/Hunt.

Baron, R. A. (1983). *Behavior in organizations: Understanding and managing the human side of work.* Boston: Allyn & Bacon.

Beehr, T. A. & Newman, J. E. (1978). Job stress, employee health, and organizational effectiveness: a facet analysis, model and literature review. *Personnel Psychology,* 31: 665-699.

Cataldo, M. F., Green, L. W., Herd, A. J., Parkinson, R. S. & Goldbeck, W. B. (1986). Preventive medicine and the corporate environment: Challenge to behavioral medicine. In M. F. Cataldo and T. J. Coates, *Health and industry: A behavioral medicine perspective.* New York: Wiley.

Cunningham, R. M., Jr. (1982). *Wellness at work*: A report on health and fitness programs for employees of business and industry. Chicago, IL: Blue Cross Association.

Debats, K. (1981). Industrial recreation programs: A new look at an old benefit. *Personnel Journal,* August, 620-627.

Everly, G. S., Jr. (1985). The foundation of occupational health promotion. In *Occupational health promotion: Health behavior in the workplace,* G. S. Everly and R. H. L. Feldman, eds., New York: Wiley.

Finney, C. (1985). Further evidence: Employee recreation and increased performance. *Employee Services Management,* 28(8), 8-10.

Grossman, J. (1981). Inside the wellness movement. *Health,* 10-15.

Hayes, M. (1986). The crisis in health care costs. *Personnel Administrator,* 31(7), 56-62, 126-130.

Hellriegel, D., Slocum, J.W. Jr., & Woodman, R.W. 1989. 5th edition. *Organizational Behavior.* St. Paul, MN:West.

Henemen, H. G., Schwab, D. P., Fossum, J. A. & Dyer, L. D. (1986). *Personnel/human resource management* (3rd edition). Homewood, IL: Irwin.

James, F. E. (1987). Study lays groundwork for tying health costs to worker's behavior. *The Wall Street Journal,* April 14, 35.

Kahn, R.L. (1981). *Work and health.* New York: Wiley.

Laughlin, J. A. (1982). Wellness at Work: A seven-step "dollars and sense" approach. *Occupational Health and Safety,* 30(11), 9-11.

McKenna, J.F., Oritt, P.L., & Wolf, H.K. (1981). Occupational stress as a predictor in the turnover decision. *Journal of Human Stress*, 12-17.

Miller, N.E. (1983). Behavioral medicine: Symbiosis between laboratory and clinic. *Annual Review of Psychology*, 34, 1-31.

Quick, J.C., & Quick, J.D. (1984). *Organizational stress and preventive management*. New York: McGraw-Hill.

Schott, F. W. (1984). WELCOM: The wellness council of the midlands. *Wellness Perspectives*, 1(3), 7-12.

Schuler, R. S. (1987). *Personnel and human resource management* (3rd edition). St. Paul, MN: West.

Seyle, H. (1974). *Stress without distress*. Philadelphia, PA: J.B. Lippincott.

Shinew, K. J. & Crossley, J. C. (1989). A comparison of employee recreation and fitness programs. *Employee Services Management*, 32(4), 26-29.

Sloan, R. P., Gruman, J. C. & Allegrante, J. P (1987). *Investing in employee health*. San Francisco, CA: Jossey-Bass.

Steers, R.M., & Rhodes, S.R. (1978). Major influences on employee attendance: A process model. *Journal of Applied Psychology*, 63, 391-407.

Streitz, T. M. (1986). The employee perspective. *Employee Services Management*, 29(5), 9-10.

Townes, C. D. (1984). Wellness: The emerging concept and its components. *Journal of Adlerian Behavior*, 6(2), 373-383.

Trenk, B. S. (1989). Corporate fitness programs become health investments. *Management Review*, 78(8), 33-37.

3

Needs Assessment

Introduction

As discussed in Chapter 2, the mission of employee services and recreation provides direction in the provision of programs. While certain outcomes or benefits are desired by organizations through the provision of employee services and recreation programs, one must assume that employees' attitudes and behaviors will change only to the extent that those services are personally meaningful to them. To be effective, employee services must address the real concerns and interests of the employees. The identification of employee concerns and interests is the primary function of the needs assessment. Managers in leisure service organizations have reported that the determination of constituent needs was one of the most important functions of their work and required a great deal of their time and attention (Busser & Bannon, 1987).

Needs assessment is defined as an applied research process for gathering data useful for individual and group planning purposes. Needs assessment is important for a variety of reasons. First, needs assessment provides a logical starting point for the development of employee service and recreation programs. The content of employee programs should not be determined solely by the budget or what was done in the past, but should be based on the results of an assessment of the needs of the employees. Without a needs assessment, programs and services are provided on the intuitive basis of what are believed to be the employees' needs, without verification of those assumptions. Successful programs must keep in mind the employee's perspective. A program that focuses on real needs is perceived by employees as a sincere effort to improve their own and their families' well-being (Garzona, 1989).

Second, needs assessment allows the programmer to investigate comprehensively the full range of interests, concerns, and attitudes of the employees, rather than narrowly defining their perceived needs. Creative, visionary programming is much more likely to evolve from such a comprehensive, inclusive assessment. Comprehensive needs assessment allows programmers to identify and target program components based on the salient priorities of their employees. This comprehensive needs assessment provides the foundation for the establishment of programs whose scope and services are broadly, rather than narrowly, defined.

In the literature, the discussion of needs can be confusing. Often the terms "needs," "wants," "interests" and "desires" are used interchangeably. This fosters difficulty in understanding and defining the concept of need. Because of this conceptual confusion, it becomes difficult to determine whether needs are accurately assessed and satisfied through programs and services. For the purpose of our discussion of needs assessment, we will distinguish between *service needs* and *service demands*. Service needs are those that employees identify and that require a resolution of a recreation, fitness, or health problem. This would involve the filling of a gap between the present condition and what is desired. Service demands are those programs that employees require in order to perform and resolve a service problem, as well as the employees' wants or desires that would contribute to greater satisfaction with the service provided. In other words, service demands move beyond the absolving of problems into a higher level of need satisfaction.

There are a variety of types of information that can be collected through a needs assessment. The information sought should be germane to the goals of the needs assessment. Without articulated goals, the program planner is left with little direction regarding the type of needs assessment information that should be collected. For example, one employee association, whose discount program became too unwieldy, utilized a needs assessment to determine which discounts were most popular and the best method of communicating their availability to employees. In addition, the association was interested in determining the most beneficial discounts and the amount of savings due to discounts (Kynkor, 1988). Another employee association used a needs assessment to determine the extent to which employees were satisfied with the overall efforts of the association and to solicit suggestions for future programs and services currently not provided. These two needs assessments requested different types of information from employees. Careful thought should be given to the intended use of the information that one collects so that employees are not providing information that is useless for your purposes.

Employees providing responses to needs assessments will have high expectations that the information disclosed will result in the provision of programs and services and that delivery issues will be resolved. The program planner should be aware of the power a needs assessment exerts in raising the expectations of employees and be careful only to elicit information that will be acted upon.

Areas of Needs Assessment

There are eight major categories of information that can be collected through a needs assessment. Each of these will be presented below, along with a brief description of the category.

Demographic Data

This includes all relevant information regarding the demographics of employees. Demographic data includes age, gender, marital status, residential location, number of family members living at home, number and ages of children, work shift, and job classification. Demographic data is useful for constructing a profile of the needs for particular groups of employees. For example, single employees may be interested in fitness activities, while employees with children may desire family programs. This information can be used to focus program development on the needs of that particular audience.

User Participation Patterns or Current Levels of Use

This category assesses the current frequency of participation in existing employee services and recreation programs. These data are useful in determining participation trends, i.e., examining if existing programs and services are under- or over-utilized, given the allocated resources, and tracking changes in participation from year to year. Additionally, this information is valuable when one is faced with the need to purchase additional equipment or to justify requests for the addition of facilities. Registration data often is utilized to construct participation trends. However, the patterns of facility and equipment use usually are not contained in registration data.

Attitudes of Employees

It is essential to identify the attitudes and beliefs of employees regarding salient aspects of program provision. Attitudes are the employees' feelings related to the importance of various issues or services. An individual's attitude towards something will affect the individual's subsequent behavior. Addressing employees' attitudes, such as the value they place on family programs, childcare, eldercare, and the opportunity to socialize with fellow employees, could be explored. The determination of these attitudes may be beneficial in setting objectives and establishing priorities for the employee services and recreation department.

Barriers to Participation

Barriers to participation are the constraints that employees perceive as preventing their participation in programs or utilization of services. One significant barrier to participation revolves around employees' lack of awareness or knowledge that a program or service exists. Other potential barriers include work schedules, family responsibilities, lack of interest, and lack of convenience. If these and similar perceived barriers to participation are not explored in a needs assessment, the programmer cannot resolve those issues that may prevent employees from involvement in programs and services, thereby reducing the effectiveness of the employee association.

Predictions of Future Participation

Sometimes the programmer is not interested in what the employees want in the present, but is instead more concerned with long-term planning. In situations such as this, the respondents may be asked to project what they perceive to be their future needs. This is a very useful category of need identification when equipment purchases are being considered, facilities are to be constructed, or contractual arrangements are being deliberated to supplement the existing services and programs.

Appraisal of Existing Facilities and Programs

Employees may be afforded the opportunity to rate the quality of existing facilities, services, and programs. This provides feedback and evaluation data so that appropriate changes can be made. In addition, this information provides insight into the current level of employee satisfaction with the association.

Health Hazard Appraisal

Health hazard appraisals are standardized instruments used to evaluate the current health status of employees and estimate the presence of potential risk factors that are predictors for disease. Risk factors include smoking, stress, family history of disease, high blood pressure, high cholesterol, and poor nutrition. The health hazard appraisal evaluates a respondent's risks compared to national statistics on the causes of death, the employee's medical history, and lifestyle. Comparisons are then made with others in the same age and gender group (Caudron, 1989). Specific recommendations can be made to an employee as a result of this evaluation. Results can also indicate potential areas for the development of services and programs.

Areas for Improvement

This component of a needs assessment provides employees with the opportunity to share suggestions or issues related to the association and its programs, services, facilities, policies, and procedures. This willingness to go to the employees for their opinions fosters a dialogue, which indicates a commitment on the part of the association to resolve problems and to provide quality programs.

Collecting Data on Needs

There are many research methods available that can be utilized to collect data on needs. The use of research methods to conduct a needs assessment requires specific knowledge and skills in order to ensure that the data collected is valid and reliable. The validity of a needs assessment refers to the degree to which the information collected accurately portrays the needs of employees. For example, a needs assessment that focused only on satisfaction with special events is not a valid assessment of overall satisfaction with employee services and should not be used as such. A poorly conceptualized needs assessment procedure truly may be measuring nothing well, and it is therefore not valid.

Reliability is concerned with the consistency of the data. Consistency indicates that the information obtained through the assessment truly represents the employees' perspective and is not influenced by outside factors, which may vary. For example, a needs assessment that asks for overall program satisfaction may get different responses if conducted in the summer versus the winter, especially if there is a strong summer activities program and nothing in the winter. If what the planner wants to determine is comprehensive levels of satisfaction, the reliability of this assessment is doubtful.

While several methods of data collection are appropriate for needs assessment, this section will describe five that are easily incorporated within the corporate setting. Three of these methods, advisory boards, key informants, and focus groups, are particularly useful in providing preliminary insights into issues, problems, concerns, and areas for needs assessment. These insights may be investigated further through more in-depth types of data collection, such as interviews and surveys.

Advisory Boards

An advisory board consists of approximately seven members who volunteer, are elected, or are appointed to serve as employee representatives of the entire corporation. The functions of an advisory board include (1) providing an opportunity for employees to participate in the decision-making process, (2) assisting in fund-raising events, (3) providing a source of volunteers, and (4) assisting the employee services and recreation staff in aligning the programs and services provided with employee needs (Kraus & Curtis, 1986).

For the purpose of needs assessment, these individuals serve the function of providing input with regard to the needs of employees for programs and services. They can be utilized as a sounding board to discuss issues, bring suggestions from employees, and assist in supporting the role of employee services and recreation departments. They also provide an additional vehicle to communicate with the employees. If employee services and recreation is formed as an association, the board of directors can fulfill this advisory role.

Key Informants

Key informants are individuals who have the knowledge and ability to report on employee needs. Key informants may be opinion leaders in the corporation who are aware of the program and service needs that are perceived as important by employees (McKillip, 1987). Advisory boards may be utilized to identify ten to fifteen key informants who are able to express their perceptions of employee needs (Gilmore, Campbell, & Becker, 1989).

Key informants are selected on the basis of (1) whether persons' views and actions influence others, (2) their level of knowledge regarding the corporation, and (3) their level of knowledge about the employee services and recreation department/association ("How to Use the Key Informant Survey Technique," 1985). Information obtained from key informants may cover the broad range of general and specific needs assessment areas. Information may be collected from key informants through an interview or survey.

Focus Groups

The use of focus groups is designed to provide general insights into the motives and behaviors of individuals through the use of unstructured interviews (Assael, 1984). The group consists of between five and twelve employees who have back-grounds or characteristics that are representative of the employ-ees throughout the corporation. A range of ages, males and females, employees with varying family configurations, i.e., single and married with children, should be depicted in the focus group as they are depicted in the workplace.

The focus group is directed by a leader, who acts as a moderator, toward understanding employee issues or needs related to the provision of programs and services. The moderator directs the session by asking questions to solicit group reactions to issues of concern. Focus group sessions are approximately two hours in duration and may be taped for later analysis of the discussion. The intent of the focus group is to generalize areas of need from the group to the larger employee base (Dignan & Carr, 1987).

Interviews

The personal interview is a face-to-face interpersonal situation in which an interviewer asks employees questions designed to obtain answers relevant to the needs assessment (Nachmias & Nachmias, 1987). A scheduled interview with structured questions has the most advantages for gaining useable information. Structured refers to questions that are the same in wording and sequence for each interviewee. Questions are written prior to the interview, and identical ones are asked in every employee interview.

The structured interview has several advantages over other methods of collecting data. Great flexibility can be used in the questioning process to probe areas of concern to the associa-tion or employees. In addition, the response rate is generally high with this method as opposed to the survey. The disadvan-tage of an interview is its higher cost and time involved in collecting the information. Interviewers also have to be trained in the techniques of effective interviewing. One final obstacle to this method is its lack of anonymity for the respondents. That is, employees who participate in the interview recognize that their identities are known by the interviewer. This may prevent the use of interviews if the information to be collected is sensitive to the employee.

Surveys

Surveys provide the greatest opportunity to solicit employee input and to generalize the findings from a smaller group of employees to the corporation as a whole. Surveys require expertise from knowledgeable individuals in order to implement them successfully. The use of company marketing departments could be extremely beneficial to most employee associations conducting surveys. There are five steps in the survey process and these include (1) an operational definition of the purpose of the survey, (2) the design and pre-testing of data collection instruments (i.e., the questionnaire or the interview guide), (3) the selection of an employee sample, (4) the data collection, and (5) an analysis of the data (York, 1982). The purpose of the survey has already been discussed in this chapter. Each additional step in the survey process will be briefly described below.

The design of the questionnaire includes the development of the specific questions to be answered by employees and decisions concerning their form (e.g., multiple choice, fill in the blank). In addition, the directions for completing the survey, the procedures for carrying out the survey, and the method of returning completed questionnaires are determined. Pre-testing the data collection instrument is essential in order to uncover or eliminate any difficulties that may exist in the data collection procedure (Bannon, 1978). Pre-tests can be considered mini-surveys and are conducted with a small group of employees who are administered the questionnaire and who identify any difficulties in understanding directions, questions, or the type of information solicited. Further, the survey process is actually tested to determine if there are any problems requiring changes.

Sampling is the use of particular procedures that allow the generalization of findings from a representative small group of employees to the whole corporate workforce. By selecting employees through a random process (e.g., selecting every tenth person from a random listing of employees), the results of the assessment are likely to be representative of the needs of all employees, even though all employees were not surveyed.

In collecting the data from employees, it is important that the cover letter of the questionnaire explain the purpose of the survey and indicate that this information is confidential. It is the ethical responsibility of those individuals conducting the survey to ensure anonymity for respondents. After the questionnaire has been sent to employees, it is important to follow up with phone calls, memos, or other methods to continue to solicit the return of surveys. To be considered sufficiently representative, at least 35% of the surveys must be completed and returned. Inducements are often used to increase the return rate. For example, the association could offer employees a discount on programs or purchases in the employee store for completing and returning the survey.

Once the data has been collected and tabulated, the data can be analyzed. The frequencies and percentages of responses to particular questions may reveal significantly desirable information. The data should be carefully analyzed to answer the questions and purpose of the survey. These results, then, become the basis for decision making, regarding the needs of employees and the programs and services provided. A sample needs assessment survey is provided in Appendix A.

Additional Sources of Assessment

There are additional sources of data that may be extremely valuable for the determination of programs and services. Specifically, company records may provide insight into the program and service needs of both the employees and the company. Employee information can be obtained from personnel records, which may highlight particular needs of the company. Records on absenteeism, sick days, and turnover may indicate areas to be addressed through the employee services and recreation program. Additionally, accident reports, medical records, and worker compensation claims could depict company trends and indicate the need for particular programs to alleviate specific employee problems. Medical screenings are also valuable sources of additional information. These may be conducted by the company through employee health fairs or corporate medical departments.

Resource Inventory

Before a program planner responds to the data generated through a needs assessment by developing programs, it is important to determine whether employees' needs can be addressed through existing community programs. A resource inventory may provide the planner with that information. A resource inventory is a compilation of the facilities, programs, and services available within the community that might be directly utilized by employees or provided through employee associations via a cooperative agreement with the community organization. This inventory becomes a directory of existing community resources related to employee services and recreation programs. Some of the information that may be collected includes (1) the sponsoring organization and eligibility requirements for participants, (2) the types of facilities, equipment, programs, and services provided, (3) the number of people served in various programs (which provides information regarding interest and demand for particular activities), (4) the cost of programs, and (5) the expertise of the staff.

The information derived from a resource inventory may be useful in determining whether programs available in the community should be duplicated by the company. It also provides insight into the cost of particular programs as an indicator for pricing decisions. In addition, a resource inventory is a valuable method of identifying organizations in the community that can support the activities of the employee services and recreation department. Soha (1988) identified a realm of potential community resources that could support current activities. These include non-profit health agencies, professional associations, government agency health resources, consumer and public safety groups, and private enterprises. Organizations in each of these areas may provide resources such as speakers, educational material, screenings, referral, training information, special programs and demonstrations. A resource inventory is a supportive document to a needs assessment. It may be as valuable to the employees as it is to staff of the employee services and recreation department.

Development of a Needs Assessment Report

A needs assessment report should be compiled and presented to management and employees. The most appropriate method of sharing this report is to compile tables, graphs, and statistics in a manner that is easily understood. It is suggested that a comprehensive report be provided to management and an executive summary to interested employees. A report should consist of the following components:

- Title page
- Executive summary
- Introduction to the needs assessment study —purpose
- Overview of methods and procedures
- Results
- Conclusions and recommendations

Summary

One of the goals of employee services and recreation departments is to achieve high levels of employee participation and satisfaction in company sponsored programs and services. In order to facilitate this goal and to act as a successful liaison between the company and employees, it is necessary to understand the current status of employee needs (Iwan, 1985). This is the vital role of the needs assessment, from which the development of programs and services emerge.

The final decision of which employee programs and services to provide is dependent on several factors, including

1. The desired outcomes for the corporation and employees,
2. The philosophy of the corporation regarding the role of employee services and recreation,
3. The resources available, in terms of corporate financial support and the facilities in-house and in the community, and
4. The information on the needs and interests of the employees, gathered through a comprehensive needs assessment (Girdano, 1986).

References

Assael, H. (1984). *Consumer behavior and marketing action* (2nd edition). Boston: Kent.

Busser, J. A. & Bannon, J. J. (1987). Work activities performed by management personnel in public leisure service organizations. *Journal of Park and Recreation Administration*, 5(1), 1-16.

Bannon, J. J. (1978). *Leisure resources: Its comprehensive planning*. Englewood Cliffs, NJ: Prentice-Hall.

Caudron, S. (1989). Health-risk assessments: Looking into your future. *Employee Services Management*, 32(3), 12-15.

Dignan, M. B. & Carr, P. A. (1987). *Program planning for health education and health promotion*. Philadelphia: Lea & Febiger.

Garzona, C. (1989). How to get employees behind your program. *Personnel Administrator*, 34(10), 60-62.

Gilmore, G. D., Campbell, M. D. & Becker, B. L. (1989). *Needs assessment strategies for health education and health promotion*. Indianapolis, IN: Benchmark.

Girdano, D. A. (1986). *Occupational health promotion: A practical guide to program development*. New York: Macmillan.

"How to Use the Key Informant Survey Technique" (1985). *How to Evaluate Education Programs*, 1-6.

Iwan, E. (1985). How to conduct an interest survey. *Employee Services Management*, 28(2), 16-19.

Kraus, R.G., & Curtis, J.E. (1986). *Creative management in recreation, parks, and leisure services*. (4th edition). St. Louis, MO: Mosby.

Kynkor, E.M. (1988). "Ring up savings:" An employee survey. *Employee Services Management*, 31(3), 21-23.

McKillip, J. (1987). *Need analysis; Tools for the human services and education*. Beverly Hills, CA: Sage

Nachmias, D. & Nachmias, C. (1987). *Research methods in the social sciences*, (3rd edition). New York: St. Martin's Press.

Soha, B. (1988). Effective use of community resources. *Employee Services Management*, 31(10), 18-21.

York, R. O. (1982). *Human service planning*. Chapel Hill, NC: The University of North Carolina Press.

4

Program Organization and Development

With the completion of an employee needs assessment, the information gathered is utilized to identify the specific programs and services needed by employees and the corporation. Once a program is identified for development, there are a variety of decisions to be rendered by the association regarding the organization of that program. This chapter will examine some of the issues in the organization and development phase of the program planning process. Specifically, the development of goals and objectives, the selection of program formats, scheduling, and the program plan will be presented.

Goals and Objectives

Once a program has been identified and selected for development, the specific program goals and objectives should be written. Goals are broad statements of program intent and provide direction toward the development of the program's content. They are not directly measurable because they are stated in broad, non-specific terms and may be idealistic (Peterson and Gunn, 1984).

Objectives are the specific, measurable outcomes of the program. Objectives state the desired result of employee involvement in the program. Objectives serve as the anchor for the design of the program; they also help guide participants toward particular outcomes. In addition, objectives provide a basis for evaluating the program. Theobald (1979) suggested the following guidelines when writing objectives: (a) objectives are stated in terms of persons involved; (b) objectives specify a behavior that can be counted, verified, or measured; and (c) objectives indicate a minimum level of accomplishment or performance.

Program Formats

Once program goals and objectives have been developed, the format of the program should be chosen. Program formats are the structures through which the activity is organized and presented (Russell, 1982). Program formats are selected on the basis of which structure provides the best method of facilitating the goals and objectives of the program. In addition, program formats play an important role in the satisfaction employees realize from participating in a program (Rossman, 1984). That is, the selection of a particular format by managers influences specific employee satisfaction with the program and the resulting experience. For example, to promote fitness, either an aerobics class or open exercise facility could be offered. The satisfaction of employees may differ depending on which of these two formats is implemented. Some formats used by associations are clubs, competitions, special events, education, and open facilities. Each format will be briefly discussed below.

Clubs

Clubs are used extensively in the corporate setting to facilitate employee involvement in association programs. The development of an employee club is initiated by employees who share common interests. Club members seek staff expertise, financial support, or other forms of assistance from the association in order to enable their participation. Clubs are developed around the common interests of employees and may be quite diverse. The different types of clubs found in employee associations focus on topics and activities such as computers, travel, sports, socializing, metallurgy, model railroads, stamps, hunting, lapidary, volunteer projects, and ceramics. Engagement in these types of clubs offers employees an opportunity to develop leisure activity skills that can be continued throughout life. Clubs are particularly important to retired employees and assist in maintaining a relationship with the company and former co-workers.

Employees often request sponsorship from the association in the form of financial support and the use of facilities and equipment. Club members may be required to develop by-laws, elect a president, submit a budget and report regularly to the association on club membership and meetings. Sample club by-laws and reporting forms (listing of assets, club officer and membership roster, monthly report, financial report) are provided in Appendix B.

Competitions

Since some employees enjoy the challenge of competition as well as the social camaraderie of team play, employee associations are often involved in the provision of recreational leagues and tournaments. Competitive events provide the opportunity for exhibition of skill, engagement in physical or mental activity with challenging opponents, and social interaction. Competitions may take various forms, such as individual, team, or corporate-wide events. Traditional tournaments also are often utilized. Tournament structures may include single and double elimination, round robin, and ladder competitions.

There are four types of tournaments that can provide some creative alternatives to traditional events. Intramural tournaments are those held within the company that provide friendly competition and fun for employees. Extramural tournaments are those held between companies that are in close proximity to each other and who may be business rivals. In charity tournaments, the proceeds of the event are donated to worthy community or national causes. Often, the charity itself sponsors and conducts the event. The corporation has an opportunity to enhance its image by endorsing and encouraging employees to participate in the event. Community tournaments are sponsored through municipal recreation departments or other community agencies. These tournaments offer employees the benefits of the correct level of competition because there are large numbers of teams involved in the leagues (Price, 1986). For example, a company might sponsor a team of its employees in a municipal softball league. A sample association policy on athletic leagues and tournaments is provided in Appendix C.

Trips and Outings

Trips and outings are becoming an increasingly popular form of employee recreation. Trips and outings require a great deal of planning and attention to detail in order to be successful. Involvement of the employee services and recreation department can range from the subsidization of tours of local attractions to the coordination of cruises and overseas tours. This format is discussed further in Chapter 6.

Special Events

Special events are the most challenging programs to run effectively, yet an extremely well-planned event can be one of the most successful and well-received programs provided through employee services and recreation departments. Special events usually stand on their own as a singular experience for the participant. Special events have a theme around which the activity is organized. They can be used effectively with many different themes, such as health fairs, craft shows, and corporate challenges. Special events are useful when initiating a new program, culminating a program, or conducting an annual event. Clubs often hold annual special events to display their accomplishments, sell products, or demonstrate skills. The goals of a special event may be varied and include educational efforts, fun and recreation, increased awareness, and development of social relationships.

Planning a special event requires careful consideration by the employee services and recreation manager. The program planner must consider numerous details regarding the event, including emergency procedures, crowd and participant control, event officials, record keeping, public address systems, food and beverage provision, and additional considerations unique to the event (Patterson, 1987).

Special events often require the programmer to secure a facility that is conducive to a successful event. Pindroh (1988) identified seven components that should be considered when selecting a facility or site for a special event. These include

1.   Type of Activity: A facility or site should be selected that

will best facilitate the accomplishment of the objectives set for the special event.

2.   Estimated Attendance: The size of a facility is a contributor to the atmosphere of the event. An overcrowded facility evokes obvious discomfort. However, one too large for the number of participants reduces the social cohesion and potential excitement of the event.

3.   Distance: One of the major factors in participation is convenience. Special events must be located within a short driving distance for employees.

4.   Safety and Security: The facility chosen should be well maintained, safe, and secure.

5.   Adequate Parking: This reduces congestion and the inconvenience of having to find a place to park or having to walk long distances.

6.   Permits and Regulations: Issues to be considered here include permits for alcoholic beverages, certificate of insurance, catering of food, and security guards.

7.   Budget Perimeters: The budget for particular special events should be in accord with the objectives for the program and the corresponding pricing perspective.

Special events require careful planning and the cooperation of all employee services and recreation staff and volunteers in order to be successful. Communication is a major factor in determining the success or failure of events. It is often helpful to have a written plan and checklist of duties for staff and volunteers. Appendix D provides a special event planning guide utilized by the 3M Club.

Education

Educational formats include workshops, seminars, clinics, and classes. The characteristics that change across these types of educational events are the nature of the material, the role of the instructor or leader, and the level of involvement of the participants. Workshops and seminars pre-suppose a high level of participant involvement; and, while the leader may be an expert on the subject, participants also share their expertise. Clinics provide training opportunities that focus on individual skill development. Classes are the most widely used format in recreation programs. This format focuses on the dissemination of information by an expert in the subject area. Classes can facilitate the acquisition of knowledge, skills, or attitudes that are related to specific activity involvement or employee lifestyle issues.

Open Facility

The provision of open facilities by an association entails making facilities and outdoor resources available for the independent involvement of the employees. It is important to allow employees the opportunity to utilize the knowledge and skills acquired through association involvement as well as to pursue individual recreational interests. Examples of open facilities include open ceramic shops, gyms, fitness equipment rooms, and an outdoor track and fitness trail.

Scheduling

In the scheduling of programs, there are several facets to consider. First, there are seasonal considerations: some programs are of interest to employees and are feasible only at certain times of the year. Second, the duration of the program should be considered. Some programs are best suited to a period of eight weeks, while others may be more appropriate for a shorter length of time. Third, the number and length of sessions are important. Most aerobics programs, for example, meet three times per week for 30 minutes. The number and length of sessions are critical factors in maintaining participant interest as well as complementing the ability of participants.

Finally, the time of day that the program will be offered needs to be determined. Most corporations allow employees to participate in association programs during non-work hours. This limits the time of day when programs may be scheduled to before and after work shifts, during lunch hours, and on weekends. The use of lunch hours for association programs may provide an opportune time to offer unique educational and learning experiences (Craig, 1987). For example, lectures, demonstrations, and films may be utilized that relate to other program areas, such as travel, fitness, or diets. Lunch-time programming can also offer a series of programs on particular topics, such as financial planning. Providing an opportunity to eat lunch during the program (e.g., brown bag) and a pleasant, relaxed atmosphere will foster participation in lunch-time offerings.

Program Plan

The manager should document the organization and development phase of the programming process in a written program plan. The program plan contains all of the elements discussed in this chapter as well as those required to implement the program. The plan serves as the basis for managing and operating the program. Included in this written document are the need for the program, goals and objectives, program format, description of program, scheduling, price, advertising and promotion, registration, staffing, equipment, supplies, and facilities required. This list of items for the program plan indicates its comprehensiveness. Once organized and developed, staff can follow the plan and implement the program as written.

Summary

This chapter provided an examination of the major tasks in the organization and development of employee programs and services. Identifying goals and objectives, the ideal program format, an appropriate schedule, and writing a comprehensive program plan are all vital to the success of these activities. Careful attention should be given to each component in this phase of the program planning process. Once the program plan is written, the tasks are carried out in the implementation phase of the program planning process. Some implementation tasks will be discussed further in Chapter 7. The following two chapters describe some of the programs and services offered by employee associations.

References

Craig, W. F. (1987). Put lunch time programs on your menu. *Employee Services Management*, 30(1), 8-12.

Patterson, F. C. (1987). *A systems approach to recreation programming.* Columbus, OH: Publishing Horizons.

Peterson, C. A. & Gunn, S. L. (1984). *Therapeutic recreation program design: Principles and practices.* Englewood Cliffs, NJ: Prentice-Hall.

Pindroh, B. (1988). Organizing special events. *Employee Services Management*, 21(1), 24-26.

Price, J. (1986). Unique tournament ideas. *Employee Services Management*, 29(2), 22-23.

Rossman, J. R. (1984). The influence of program format choice on participant satisfaction. *Journal of Park and Recreation Administration*, 2(1), 39-51.

Russell, R. V. (1982). *Planning programs in recreation.* St. Louis, MO: Mosby.

Theobald, W. F. (1979). *Evaluation of recreation and park programs.* New York: Wiley.

5

Employee Services

Employee services is an umbrella term that represents a wide range of employee benefits provided through associations. The overall intent of these services is to cater to the needs of every employee in the company by offering a variety of valuable service benefits. This chapter will describe some of the services provided through employee associations. Although not all-inclusive, these services represent some of the major undertakings currently being offered in the field.

Employee Assistance Programs (EAPs)

For many years, the personal and home life issues of employees were regarded in a hands-off approach by employers. If employees had personal problems or addictions that affected their performance, the employer would most likely terminate those employees or ignore the problem for as long as possible. Today, many companies have a different outlook and a greater range of options. Employee Assistance Programs allow a company to adopt a proactive stance towards employees' personal needs. This orientation not only allows the company to address employees' needs, but also benefits the company with a more productive and healthier workforce.

Employee Assistance Programs have helped change the perception of the workplace from the indifferent creator of stress to a possible source of help for employees' life problems. According to Masi and Friedland (1988), 18% of the average workforce have personal problems that decrease productivity. Of these affected employees, 12% have alcohol/drug-related problems, and 6% have emotionally related problems. These types of problems can impact productivity negatively by as much as 25%. Emotional problems may include difficult relationships at home or in the workplace, childrearing problems, life stressors, financial problems, depression, anxiety, and grief issues. Employee Assistance Programs are open to all employees in the workplace. Referrals can be made by an employee's supervisor, or involvement can be initiated by the employees themselves. Some Employee Assistance Programs provide services to the employees only, while other EAPs provide family services as well.

The types of services provided by EAPs vary by company. However, all EAPs provide information, assessment, and referral services. The information provided by EAPs can include materials on stress management, characteristics of addictions, common relationship and family issues, and budgeting. This information can be provided through brochures, workshops, and newsletters.

While a supervisor may be responsible for identifying an employee's productivity problem, the actual assessment of employee need is done by the EAP staff. The EAP staff determines the nature and severity of the employee's problems. This assessment may be done through standardized diagnostic instruments, interview procedures developed by the EAP staff, or a combination of the two.

Referrals can be made either to an on-site program or to a community program. Many companies provide in-house counseling services to employees. The lengths and types of counseling may vary; however, for the most part, the in-house counseling is usually short term. When the need is indicated, most EAPs use community or private resources for actual treatment. For example, employees may be referred to an inpatient chemical dependency program or to an outpatient mental health group.

Employee Assistance Programs may be very expensive to implement. It is imperative that the EAP have strong corporate backing that includes financial support for the provision of qualified staff and office space and a willingness to contribute financially to the necessary treatment of employees. Because of the cost associated with the treatment of addictions and mental health issues, many EAPs have begun to work in association with externally-managed care firms (Tune, 1988). The purpose of these firms is to manage the cases of any employees who enter an external treatment setting in order to 1) determine whether employees are receiving quality care that addresses their needs, and 2) keep the health care costs as low as possible. When an externally-managed care firm is handling a case, that firm monitors the employee's progress and determines when the employee's needs have been adequately met. This type of managed care removes total decision making from the treatment facilities and allows companies greater control of health care costs.

Childcare

The employee benefit of the 1990s may very well be childcare (Dewsnap & Cramer, 1985). Almost half of the current workforce is female, and 90% of female workers will have children while employed (Werther, 1989). Approximately 50% of the women in the labor force have infants or toddlers (Dewsnap & Cramer, 1985). The availability and quality of childcare is a concern of these families, and the willingness of a corporation to address these concerns may impact the attitudes and behaviors of their current and future employees.

Various benefits to the corporation may result from the provision of childcare services to employees. Among these are reduced turnover among staff, reduced absenteeism and tardiness, improved productivity, and higher morale. A reduction in turnover among employees impacts the corporation by reducing recruitment expenses, such as advertising and interviewing. Training costs of new employees are also lessened (Levine, 1989). Many companies use the availability of childcare services as a recruitment tool, which may be increasingly important as the labor pool shrinks and more women enter the work force. Absenteeism is a significant problem for many corporations. According to Levine (1989), one company that instituted a childcare program reported a reduction in employee absences of 15,000 hours during the first year of the program. Improved productivity and morale have also been associated with the provision of childcare services. Employees who are worried about their children's welfare, who may be supervising "latch-key" children at home by phone, or who have undependable childcare providers are less likely to be giving their full attention to their work responsibilities. Employees are also more likely to be loyal and invested in a corporation that is concerned about the quality of their family life.

Various forms of childcare assistance may be provided by employee services. Each of these forms will be discussed below.

Corporate Daycare

On-site or near-site daycare facilities may be provided by a single corporation or in conjunction with other local companies as a consortium. The corporation may provide start-up costs and then subsidize the center or provide initial costs and expect the daycare center to support itself through user fees. These centers must meet all local licensing requirements for both facilities and staffing (Werther, 1989).

Expansion of Community Daycare

Corporations can also band together to raise funds for the expansion of already existing daycare facilities in the community that might meet the needs of their employees. Alternatively, corporations may be able to influence a potential daycare provider to build a daycare center close to their site, especially if it receives corporate funding to offset start-up expenses.

Corporate Discounts

Some corporations provide employees with vouchers or corporate discounts for childcare costs. With the voucher system, the corporation would pay a portion of the childcare expenses either directly to the provider or through payroll deductions. In addition, corporate discounts may be arranged with established daycare centers in the community (Levine, 1989).

Salary Reductions

Salary reductions may be provided through which childcare expenses of up to $5,000 annually can be deducted from the employee's pay prior to taxation. These salary reductions would reduce the taxes that the employees pay and, therefore, would increase their take-home pay. An additional advantage to the corporation is that the employer also receives tax reductions from the program (Werther, 1989).

Information and Referral

Childcare information and referral programs are offered by many corporations. Services that corporations may provide include resource information on available community childcare, selection criteria for quality daycare programs, parenting workshops, and employee support groups (Briestensky, 1984).

Organizational Policies

Flextime and job sharing are organizational policies that enable employees to provide childcare for their own children. Under a flextime schedule, the employees work at crucial work times; however, they have some latitude around less crucial work times. For example, employees may choose to start their workday at 10:00 a.m. rather than 8:30 a.m. In the case of job sharing, two employees may choose to share a position, with some reduction in full-time benefits, in order to spend time with their children.

Parental leave or family sick time are also organizational policies that may benefit employees with childcare needs. Parental leave allows a parent time off after the birth or adoption of a child. This time can be either paid or unpaid. Family sick time allows a parent to take time off to spend with a sick family member. Family sick time is granted in addition to the standard sick leave for employees (Werther, 1989).

Eldercare

An employee service that will receive increasing attention in the future is that of eldercare. People over the age of 85 represent the fastest growing segment of the population (Werther, 1989). As people live longer, the responsibility of their care often falls on the shoulders of their children. In a study conducted by the Travelers Companies, it was reported that 52% of the caregivers of aging relatives were in the 41-55 age group (Pfeiffer & Silveous, 1989). Employers are noting that caregivers of aging individuals are more likely to have excessive personal phone calls on company time, higher absenteeism and tardiness, more frequent complaints of stress, and reduction in productivity (Tober, 1987).

Corporations have begun to implement services and programs designed to offer some help or support to these employees. There are corporations that currently provide their employees with resource information and free consultations and referrals in areas such as selecting a home-health nurse, adult daycare opportunities for aging individuals, nursing home placement, meal delivery services, and home maintenance and repair services for the aging. Some corporations offer their employees personal leave in order to care for an aging relative, although the leave is usually unpaid. There are also examples of companies within a community establishing a non-profit organization to provide both direct services and referral services to the elderly relatives of employees. These services include respite care, homemakers, and home-delivered meals (Werther, 1989). Informational workshops and counseling also are offered in order to meet this area of employee need.

Startup Kits

The American Association of Retired Persons has developed a program kit to assist caregivers entitled "Caregivers in the Workplace." The program kit includes information for organizing eldercare services and a sample needs assessment survey for determining the issues of interest to and services required by caregiving employees. Southwestern Bell Telephone Company also has developed a caregiving program kit. Targeted to professionals, community organizations, and employers, the kit includes a 28-minute video that includes practical information about available resources, a manual for developing eldercare programs, and an audiotape for those unable to attend special seminars on caregiving and eldercare (Azarnoff, 1988).

Pre-retirement Programs

For many employees, retirement brings with it mixed feelings. While employees may look forward to the time when their life and schedule is not tied to the workplace, retirement also presents many changes. Employers are increasingly offering pre-retirement planning programs in order for employees to make this transition as comfortable and rewarding as possible. Pre-retirement programs are designed to provide their employees with retirement information, an awareness of possible issues that they might face, and options and alternatives that they can explore (Corbett, 1989).

Effective pre-retirement programming is not conducted in the months immediately prior to retirement but instead is offered during the ten to fifteen years before employees are scheduled to retire. This time lag allows employees to plan for any contingencies they may have overlooked in their own personal planning. The content of pre-retirement planning may cover many topics, and both in-house and outside experts may be utilized in the provision of the program.

The topics that have been traditionally offered through pre-retirement programming are as follows (McFadden, 1985):

* The benefits offered by the company, such as pensions and health insurance, are discussed. It is important that the employees make an accurate estimate of the amount of retirement income they will derive from work-related sources.

* Financial planning is also an essential component of pre-retirement programming. Budgeting for retirement, investments such as stocks in solid companies or certificates of deposit, inflation factors that might impact their real incomes, and social security are all important topics to be addressed.

* Health, safety, and lifestyle concerns, such as health screenings, nutrition, suitable exercise, weight control, and the physical changes associated with aging, can all have implications for not only the length of life, but also the quality of that life.

*   A discussion of legal issues, such as wills and estate planning, is relevant for those approaching retirement age.

*   Some retirees may experience a loss of identity as they make the transition from worker to retiree. They may face a plethora of time and not know how to fill it with meaningful, rewarding experiences. Some individuals may benefit from the incorporation of volunteer work, which utilizes their work skills and retains their status of being a productive individual. Others may benefit from the identification of leisure attitudes and activities that they could cultivate and enjoy in retirement.

Employee Store

The employee store functions to provide employees with products and services at substantial savings. It also is intended to provide employees with a convenient place to shop. In addition, the company can use the store as an avenue to familiarize employees with company products (e.g., models of airplanes produced by an airline manufacturer could be sold in the store). The employee store also can market products that include the company logo. The company logo can be placed on a vast array of quality products grouped under the general categories of personal items, clothing, jewelry, and business items (Loftice, 1986). Some popular examples include

Personal items:	*Clothing:*
Coffee mugs	T-shirts
Glasses	Sweat suits
Coasters	Jackets
Key chains	Emblems
Money clips	Golf caps
Jewelry:	*Business items:*
Tie tacs, bars	Pens
Lapel pins	Note pads
Earrings	Clipboards
Watches	Business card holders
Necklaces	Employee ID holders

These types of products are very desirable to an employee if the employee feels positively towards the company. They benefit the company by embodying a spirit of pride and sense of belonging. Company employees should be consulted when determining the products to be sold in the store in order to ensure that the venture meets employee needs and is successful.

While the intent is to make the employee store a source of savings for the employee, it is also a viable method for generating income that can be utilized to support other areas of the employee services and recreation program. For example, fair trade items, those that can be purchased at other stores, can include a markup of 10%-12%. Specialty items with the company logo can be priced at 40% over cost, as they are unobtainable elsewhere. If the purpose of the employee store is to generate income to support other programs, and employee services and recreation is under a non-profit association, the association may wish to establish an employee store as a for-profit subsidiary. Company lawyers and accountants may be able to provide advice regarding liability and taxation for incorporating the employee store as a profit- making subsidiary of the association (Schools, 1984).

Discounts

One of the primary endeavors of many employee associations is the provision of employee discounts. Employee discounts provide employees with reductions in the price of products, services, and events. These savings are much greater than what an individual could arrange independently. The corporation has the advantage of presenting a large pool of prospective buyers; therefore, the manufacturer or distributor may be more willing to negotiate price reductions. Providing discount savings at area attractions can positively impact the leisure of employees and their families (Marks, 1989). There are different types of employee discounts, which can be grouped under five categories:

* Discounts are available on products, such as magazines, appliances, computers. These can be offered through the association or directly from the manufacturer or distributor.

     * Membership cards are discount opportunities provided by the attractions themselves. For example, a group of hotels, restaurants, and outdoor attractions in a certain locale may offer a packet of discounts ranging from 10% to 20% in order to attract patrons. Individual attractions, such as Disneyland, offer their own discount cards. Membership cards are available to corporations, depending on the number of employees.
     * An employee association can obtain consignment tickets from an attraction or event. A consignment agreement between the association and the ticket seller allows the association to reimburse the seller for the cost of tickets after they have been sold to the employees. The advantage of a consignment system is that the employee association can broker ticket sales without using its own capital.
     * Employee associations also can purchase bulk tickets from a local theater and sell them to their employees at savings of up to 50%. Tickets are usually purchased in large quantities, e.g., 1000 tickets, and there is sometimes an expiration date on the tickets or restrictions on the days and times they can be used.
     * Reserve tickets can be purchased to obtain excellent seating to events, such as theater productions, concerts and sporting events. The association purchases the tickets in advance, usually in increments of two. These tickets cannot be returned to the distributor, although the association may assist employees in reselling their tickets if they are unable to use them at the time of the event. Reserve ticket savings to the employees can amount to $5.00 per ticket. In addition, particular events may be subsidized by the employee association, which increases the savings to employees.

Travel Services

     Employee associations can offer travel services on a variety of levels, ranging from day trips to local destinations to extensive tour programs. The key to the success of any travel endeavor is excellent planning, marketing and follow-through. When employee associations first get involved in the provision of travel services, it is a good idea to start small and do a thorough assessment of employee interests and needs. One fundamental skill that must be learned is the vocabulary of the travel industry. Price (1986) provides a glossary of travel terms that is particularly useful as an orientation to the employee services manager who wishes to become involved in travel planning.

Employee associations that want to begin providing travel services to their employees can begin with day trips. Day trips usually require that the organizer is able to identify local or regional attractions, such as outdoor areas, cultural events, or sporting events, that a group of employees may have an interest in attending. The employee association keeps an ongoing current list of such opportunities and assesses the interests of employees for involvement. The organizer can provide employees with information on the upcoming opportunity, promote the travel experience, and arrange transportation for the outing. The employee association also arranges for the purchase of tickets or reservations, if they are necessary.

Weekend getaways are becoming more popular among employees (Sweigert, 1988). Weekend getaways allow the employees to experience special travel events periodically throughout the year rather than waiting for their annual vacation. According to Harris (1987), these mini-vacations contribute to greater efficiency in employees, reduced stress throughout the work year, group cohesiveness among fellow travelers, and increased employee morale and company loyalty.

When planning a weekend jaunt for employees, no more than six hours should be spent in getting to the location. Employees should be able to leave by bus on Friday after work; for example, arrive Friday night, and be home by 11:00 p.m. Sunday evening (Harris, 1987). Almost two full days should be spent at the location chosen. With the ready availability of flights to various destinations, possible locations for mini-vacations are virtually limitless.

Examples of possible ideas for mini-vacations (Harris, 1987) include

* bicycle, hiking, backpacking, or canoeing excursions
* ski trips
* shopping trips
* theater packages
* gambling junkets

* resorts
* festivals and cultural events
* out-of-town sporting events

The most challenging type of travel service to provide is the tour (Angersbach, 1989). The planning that goes into providing a successful tour is extensive and includes such things as arranging flights, lodging, and meals; scheduling and orchestrating all events; arranging for a tour guide who is knowledgeable about the destination, and considering liability and budgeting concerns. Because of the difficulty of organizing and facilitating a successful tour, the employee association may want to work with tour companies. Not only do tour companies have the expertise necessary to conduct a successful tour, but also they are usually able to secure a better price for accommodations and tickets. A good tour company can save the association both time and money. However, these trips require long-range planning in order for employees to schedule vacation time.

Any time that an employee association is working with outside companies, such as tour and bus companies, the association should receive a contract detailing exactly what services are to be provided and at what cost. When working with a tour company, ensure that the company has both "adequate insurance and carries an errors and omissions policy" (Harris, 1987).

With tours, as with all other types of travel services, the association must promote the travel experience. Associations can market their available travel packages in a number of ways, including tour company presentations of destinations, employee newsletter announcements, poster and video presentations of destinations, and theme days at work in which employees are invited to wear the cultural dress of the destination site, e.g., Mexico or Hawaii, and the cafeteria serves food from that locale.

As with all employee services, evaluation is an essential part of determining participant response to the experience. Participants may simply be asked to complete an evaluation form for the association, or the association may conduct a post-trip social in which all of the participants, and anyone else who is interested, can get together and show slides, have refreshments, and evaluate the trip. This gathering may be useful to the association in getting ideas for and promoting future trips as well as in facilitating interest on the part of others in the next planned excursion.

Community Service Projects

Most corporations recognize that their relationship with the community is an important one. Corporations believe that community service enhances the image of the company, improves employee morale and camaraderie, and enables them to become full partners in their communities by returning something of value. Some examples of company involvement include providing financial support to non-profit organizations or matching any employee contributions, implementing community projects, providing volunteers for community programs with salary reimbursement by the company, loaning administrators to serve non-profit organizations, and donating materials or services (Kelley, 1989).

It is important for companies to be directly involved in both the recruitment and reinforcement of employees for community service. For example, when a company solicits volunteers, there is approximately a 60% participation rate; employee involvement drops to only 39% when the company is not involved (*Newsweek*, 1988). Associations should also recognize the contributions of their employees. Some possible means of reinforcing community service are letters of appreciation; certificates, plaques, or other commemorative items; acknowledgement in the company newspaper, and formal recognition at company banquets.

Photo Processing

Photo processing is one of the easiest employee services to administer — as many as 80 percent of employees may utilize this service (Price, 1986). The reasons for high employee participation are twofold: convenience and cost savings. Depending on market conditions, employees may save from 20 - 50 percent of the cost of processing their film. Contingent on the size of the company, either a direct mail service or a pick up and delivery method can be implemented. The latter is preferred because it reduces the turnaround time for the completion of the film processing. Whichever method is utilized, employees need only deposit their film at a drop box and then return for pick-up. Photo processing is provided at either a self-service station or as part of the employee store. Photo processing has the additional benefit to the association of being a good way of generating income to offset the costs of other activities.

Hotel Guide

Hotels are increasingly providing fitness amenities in order to meet the needs of their patrons. An association can compile a directory of recommended hotels (e.g., Marriott, Sheraton, Westin, Hilton, Hyatt, and Holiday Inn) and list the fitness and recreation amenities available. If hotels are unable to provide their own facilities, they are increasingly developing cooperative agreements with local health and fitness clubs, which allow hotel guests to work out for free or a nominal fee (Robinson, 1985). The association's hotel directory provides employees with the opportunity to make travel and hotel arrangements that allow the continuation of light exercise workouts while out of town. Information contained in the directory would include the types of workout equipment available at hotels, for example, stationary bicycles, weight rooms, rowing machines, swimming pools, aerobic classes, whirlpools, walking trails, and tennis courts.

Travel and Exercise Kit

A travel and exercise kit is designed to be checked out by employees to facilitate the continuation of their health and fitness exercise program when out of town and at locations where fitness equipment is unavailable. The kit may contain a hand grip, jump rope, personal home gym, pedometer, chart/guide to stretching exercises, aerobics audio tapes and tape player, exercise video tapes, a guide to low-calorie restaurant dining, and a NutraSweet calorie substitution guide. The kit may be designed to include any or all of the items the employee chooses.

Ride Sharing

Although ride sharing is not as popular as it once was, it remains a program that makes environmental, social, and economic sense. According to Churchill (1987), every new van pool that is formed replaces ten cars, saves 10,000 gallons of gasoline, and reduces air pollution by seven tons annually. Individuals who share rides are more likely to relax and visit on their way to and from work. Ride sharing saves the employee money in a number of ways, such as for gasoline expenses, parking fees, automobile maintenance costs, and insurance premiums. The benefits to the corporation include reduced absenteeism and tardiness, increased incentives for recruitment, and less stress experienced by employees upon reaching the workplace.

Corporate programs may take a number of different forms, such as the organization of car and van pools, or the subsidization of public transportation passes. Employee service programs can facilitate car pooling by promoting it through preferred parking or the waiver of parking fees and by computerizing lists that match employees on the same shift and those living near each other (Churchill, 1987). Corporations can also purchase vans to be used by employees for commuting to and from work, although the purchase and maintenance of the van fleet can become quite expensive. Lastly, employee services can pay for a portion of public transportation expenses incurred by their employees or, as part of the discount program, sell bus passes. The bus passes could be paid for through a payroll deduction program.

Health and Fitness Evaluation

The American College of Sports Medicine (1986) has established specific guidelines for determining whether individuals should participate in physical fitness and exercise programs. These guidelines recommend that individuals obtain a medical evaluation as well as a physical fitness evaluation prior to engaging in physical exercise programs, especially if the individual is 35 years of age or older. A medical evaluation is conducted by the employee's physician before the physical fitness test. The medical evaluation provides clearance for an individual to engage in fitness activities, including fitness testing, and identifies any risk factors that would prevent an individual from participating in an exercise program. The information sources for a medical evaluation include a medical history, a physical examination, and laboratory tests (Golding, Myers & Sinning, 1989). A sample retiree health information questionnaire, which is to be completed by a physician prior to the employee engaging in physical activities is provided in Appendix E.

Physical fitness evaluations frequently are offered at the worksite. These evaluations are especially useful in determining an individual's baseline level of fitness in order to prescribe an exercise regimen and set goals to increase his or her health. In addition, physical fitness evaluations afford the opportunity to motivate individuals to exercise, and they assist in monitoring an employee's progress toward a healthier profile. An example form for prescribing employee fitness activities and monitoring progress is provided in Appendix F. An employee should be informed of the inherent risks and benefits of these evaluation procedures and sign a liability waiver (Patton, Corry, Gettman & Graf, 1987). Physical fitness evaluations usually test four major components of health, including cardiovascular endurance, muscular strength and endurance, muscular flexibility, and body composition (Hoeger, 1988). The evaluation of these four components of fitness should be conducted by qualified personnel.

Cardiovascular Endurance

Of the four health-related components of physical fitness, cardiovascular endurance is considered the best indicator of overall health. Cardiovascular fitness is "the ability of the heart, blood vessels, blood, and respiratory system to supply fuel, especially oxygen, to the muscles during sustained exercise" (Corbin & Lindsey, 1985; p. 8). An individual with good cardiovascular endurance can continue exercising for long periods of time without undue stress. Cardiovascular endurance can be measured by three common methods: (1) the time it takes to run 1.5 miles, (2) the three-minute step test, and (3) the Astrand-Ryhmig test, which uses a bicycle ergometer. Each of these could be administered at the worksite.

Muscular Strength

Muscular strength and endurance are important components of health and are necessary to function in daily life. Activities such as running, walking, sitting, lifting, and carrying objects require muscular strength and endurance. There are two major benefits of muscular strength and endurance. Strengthening various muscle groups helps prevent posture problems and low back pain. Also, by developing the size of muscles or muscle mass, an individual's resting metabolism is increased. That is, increasing muscle mass increases the calories burned while at rest. Muscular strength and endurance can be easily measured through a variety of tests, such as the hand grip dynamometer, the bench press, sit-ups, modified push-ups, and the exercise stations found on the Universal Gym apparatus.

Muscular Flexibility

Muscular flexibility is the range of possible movement in a joint (e.g., knee) or series of joints (e.g., spinal column). Muscular flexibility reduces the incidence of low back and spinal column problems, improves posture, and facilitates the development and maintenance of motor skills throughout life. The use of stretching exercises also prepares the body for more rigorous exercise. The Sit-and-Reach test has been frequently used as a measure of overall flexibility. However, flexibility is specific to each of the body's joints, and as a result, there is no single test of muscular flexibility.

Body Composition

Body composition refers to the determination of fat and lean tissue or muscle of the human body. The purpose of this fitness test is to identify the percentage of body fat in relation to an individual's weight. A target range for percentage of body fat is 15% for men and 20% for women. Body composition may be determined accurately through three methods. These include (1) hydrostatic weighing, which involves the immersion of an individual underwater, (2) electrical impedance, which uses a weak bio-electrical current to measure the resistance to electrical flow, and (3) skinfolds, which measure the thickness of the fat found directly under the skin at various body sites. Hydrostatic weighing can be accomplished at the worksite with portable tanks. However, the other two methods are easier to administer.

Fitness Trail

A fitness trail is a self-guided series of fitness stations that may incorporate fitness testing along with an exercise conditioning program. Self-tests measure each component of total fitness, including cardiovascular endurance, flexibility, muscular endurance and strength. Employees conduct self-tests utilizing guidelines provided at each station and then record their scores. This provides baseline data so that individuals may keep track and record their progress in each area of fitness.

When looking for an appropriate set of fitness stations, Bower (1985) suggested paying attention to the exercise routines. Specifically the fitness trail should provide a "sensible, well balanced, carefully designed program incorporating stretching, strengthening and cardiovascular conditioning exercises" (p. 12). The monitoring of the heartbeat should be incorporated into the exercise stations in order for participants to monitor their progress, regardless of age or fitness level.

Jogging/Walking Maps

Maps that indicate routes and distances for joggers and walkers can be developed by the association. Maps should provide an array of routes that not only are conducive to the distance needs of individual employees, but also provide variety for engaging in the activity and reducing boredom. Employees could be encouraged to submit their favorite routes.

Summary

This chapter has provided an overview and description of some of the major employee services currently being offered through associations. Several of these services represent the core of associations' efforts. That is, services such as the employee store, discounts, travel and photo processing are the basic services furnished to all employees. These services are also indicative of those that employees utilize the most.

References

American College of Sports Medicine (1986). *Guidelines for exercise testing and prescription* (3rd edition). Philadelphia, PA: Lea & Febiger.

Angersbach, G. F. (1989). Arranging tours. *Employee Services Management*, 32(8), 27-28.

Azarnoff, R. S. (1988). Can employees carry the eldercare burden? *Personnel Journal*, 67(9), 60-65.

Bower, K. (1985). Follow the trail to fitness. *Employee Services Management*, 28(9), 12-13.

Briestensky, B. A. (1984). The childcare business. *Employee Services Management*, 27(3), 20-24.

Churchill, S. M. (1987). Who's caring about ride sharing? *Employee Services Management*, 30(1), 23-24.

Corbett, C. B. (1989). Uncharted territory: Retirement. *Employee Services Management*, 22(7), 15-17.

Corbin, C. B. & Lindsey, R. (1985). *Concepts of physical fitness with laboratories* (5th edition). Dubuque, IA: Wm. C. Brown.

Dewsnap, L. & Cramer, J. (1985). Childcare comes of age. *Employee Services Management*, 28(7), 17-23.

Golding, L. A., Myers, C. R. & Sinning, W. E. (1989). *Y's way to physical fitness* (3rd edition). Champaign, IL: Human Kinetics.

Harris, N. R. (1987). Planning weekend getaways. *Employee Services Management*, 30(7), 9-14.

Hoeger, W. W. K. (1988). *Principles and labs for physical fitness and wellness*. Englewood, CO: Morton.

Kelley, M. (1989). Community service projects: Should we be involved? *Employee Services Management*, 32(9), 12-16.

Levine, R. (1989). Childcare: Inching up the corporate agenda. *Management Review*, 78(1), 43-47.

Loftice, K. (1986). Using logo items. *Employee Services Management*, 29(8), 13-14.

Marks, D. (1989). Attraction tickets. *Employee Services Management*, 32(4), 30-31.

Masi, D. A. & Friedland, S. J. (1988). EAP actions & options. *Personnel Journal*, 67(6), 61-67.

McFadden, J. J. (1985). A bridge to retirement. *Employee Services Management*, 28(5), 10-11.

Newsweek , February 8, 1988, p. 26.

Patton, R. W., Corry, J. M., Gettman, L. R. & Graf, J. S. (1986). *Implementing health/fitness programs.* Champaign, IL: Human Kinetics.

Price, J. E. (1986). Photo processing: A picture-perfect employee service. *Employee Services Management,* 29(1), 27-28.

Price, J. E. (1986). ABC's of travel planning. *Employee Services Management,* 29(2), 14-21.

Schools, R. (1984). Running the company store. *Employee Services Management,* 27(6), 14-16,18.

Sweigert, B. (1988). Planning the complete travel program. *Employee Services Management,* 31(7), 12-15.

Tober, P. (1987). Eldercare: Benefit of the 1990s. *Employee Services Management,* 30(2), 14-17.

Tune, G. F. (1988). Employee assistance: An innovative approach to EAPs and managed care. *Personnel Journal,* 67(10), 52-55.

Werther, W. B. (1989). Childcare and eldercare benefits. *Personnel,* September, 42-46.

6

Employee Programs

This chapter will highlight and describe some of the employee recreation, health, and fitness programs currently being provided in the field. These programs have been defined as activities or events in which the individuals who participate receive some benefits or satisfactions from their involvement (Rossman, 1989). In the same context as the previous chapter, these programs are not all-inclusive, but rather are major offerings and constitute a starting point for the employee services and recreation professional.

Aerobic Dance

Aerobic dance is an extremely popular fitness activity that combines exercise and dance gestures along with rhythmical step patterns and music. There are two major types of aerobic dance: high impact and low impact. Low impact has generally been endorsed as a safer exercise because people experience fewer types and numbers of related injuries. The overall goal of aerobic dance is to increase cardiovascular endurance. That is, participating in aerobic dance provides participants with fitness benefits that include increasing the efficiency of the lungs, heart, and vascular system. There are three main criteria for safe and effective aerobic dance programs, which include (1) the frequency of the sessions per week, which should be limited to every other day, (2) the intensity or how stressful the program is, which should not exceed 75% of maximal heart rate, and (3) the duration of each session, which should not exceed 30 minutes (Mazzeo & Kisselle, 1987). Aerobic dance sessions should begin with warm-up exercises to loosen muscles and end with cool-down exercises to reduce the potential for injury.

According to a recent survey of participants in aerobic dance, individuals engage in this activity primarily to stay in shape and to lose weight. These survey respondents also reported that an aerobic dance instructor with enthusiasm and motivational abilities was desirable (Davis & LeCompte, 1988). It is important to hire an aerobic dance instructor who has certified training. There are three predominant certifying organizations for aerobic dance instructors, including (1) Aerobic and Fitness Association of America, (2) International Dance and Exercise Association, and (3) American College of Sports Medicine.

Aerobic dance is only one of many fitness activities that provide aerobic benefits. Others include swimming, running, walking, cross-country skiing, rope jumping, and bicycling. Aerobic activities can be facilitated through a variety of exercise machines such as rowers, treadmills, stair climbers, and stationary bicycles. In fact, varying aerobic routines is considered to be beneficial to the participant. Labeled as cross training, changing the aerobic fitness routine potentially reduces boredom and injuries while providing a more complete workout.

Health Fair

A corporate health fair provides employees with educational information regarding health and fitness as well as medical screenings to detect indicators of poor health. Health fairs are usually well attended and serve as an excellent introduction for employees to the programs provided by the employee services and recreation department. The involvement of local health agencies, such as hospitals or medical clinics, are central to the viability of a health fair. In addition, physicians are usually willing to donate their time to such an event. Health fairs are often planned in accordance with health themes for a particular month. Information and services provided at the health fair is dependent on the needs of employees and the resources available. There are four major components that may be included in any health fair. These include exhibits, screenings, summary and referral, and follow-up services (Cato, 1988; Okerlund, 1984).

Exhibits

Exhibits can be offered on a wide range of health and fitness related subjects, including nutrition, back safety, CPR, substance abuse, strokes, muscular dystrophy, and proper safety of recreation equipment. In addition, organizations can be contacted to provide displays and may send representatives to distribute brochures containing specific health information, provide demonstrations and films, or conduct short lectures. Some organizations that may be contacted include

*American Lung Association *American Cancer Society

*American Red Cross *American Heart foundation

*Alzheimers Disease *Kidney Foundation
  Association

*National Dairy Council

Screenings

Screenings are brief health and fitness tests conducted at the health fair and are excellent methods of assessing potentially harmful situations that may put individuals at risk. Most screenings are free, except those that require laboratory work. Corporate group insurance should be contacted in order to determine if a percentage of the costs may be shared with employees. Screenings that are conducive to a health fair include those for

*blood pressure   *fitness
*diabetes   *colon rectal problems
*stress   *hearing
*glaucoma   *visual acuity
*height/weight   *blood chemistry
*breast tumors   *lead poisoning
*podiatry problems   *Tay-Sachs disease
*sickle cell trait   *oral hygiene

Summary and Referral

Summary and referral are important components of a health fair because of the complex medical issues involved. During the summary and referral phase, medical personnel advise and counsel employees pertaining to their results in order to minimize the misinterpretation of test results. Tests are reviewed with particular emphasis on risk factors of concern. Specific education for the employee is conducted in this stage and, if necessary, community medical sources are suggested for further testing.

Follow-up

Follow-up for most test results occurs immediately, with the exception of blood chemistry and cardiac profiles, which require laboratory analysis. These results are mailed to employees. It is important to conduct a follow-up with employees who receive test results at home in order to determine their understanding of the laboratory analysis. In addition, a 3-month follow-up with employees who had a health problem identified should be conducted. This may ensure that employees seek treatment and provide the status or actions taken to resolve the health problem.

Parenting Fairs

Parenting fairs are an additional way to continue to address the issues of work and family (Grumbine, 1989). Similar to health fairs, parenting fairs provide information and education on work and family issues, answer questions, and provide opportunities for referrals. Speakers may provide lectures on such topics as childcare providers, latch-key children, child development, and children's educational needs. Examples of exhibitors include

*Police Department   *Daycare centers
*Fire Department   *Services for sick children
*YMCA & YWCA   *Toy and game retailers
*Local zoo   *Art organizations
*Parks and Recreation Department   *Parent support groups
*Summer camps   *Bookstores
*Library   *Universities - childcare

Service Awards Program

The purpose of a service awards program is to recognize the effort and dedication of employees who have chosen to remain with the company. Service awards are a motivational tool that reward employees at specific length-of-service increments. The most widely-used service awards include jewelry, plaques, watches and clocks, pins, crystal/glassware, pen and pencil sets, cash, certificates, selection from a gift catalogue, U.S. savings bonds, and dinners. One factor that is relevant for the motivational effect of service awards is that rewards must be valued by the individual. Recognizing the importance of valuing rewards, an assortment of service award items can be offered at particular anniversary mileposts (e.g., 5 years, 10 years) from which employees may choose. In this way, employees can select the award that is most meaningful to them from a gift catalogue. Another important component of a service awards program is the role that management plays in recognizing employees. It may be helpful for managers to prepare small fact cards that list the employee's first assignment, special achievements, hobbies, and interests (Walsh, 1989).

Walking Program

Walking is one of the most popular fitness activities in the country, with over 50 million Americans participating. Cooper (1983) rates walking as one of the five major aerobic exercises. Aerobic exercise improves cardiovascular conditioning, and in fact, walking produces approximately the same overall benefits as jogging. The only drawback is the longer period of time required to receive benefits from walking as opposed to jogging (Sweetgall, 1986). However, walking is a safe and effective method of increasing health especially for those employees over 50 years of age. Hamman (1989) suggests the following benefits of participating in a walking program on a regular basis.

*   Takes very little equipment to develop or participate in a walking program.

*   Encourages all forms of participation. A participant can walk almost anywhere, with or without a group, at work or at home.

*   Allows all fitness levels and abilities a chance to participate.

*   Promotes an exercise people can do for a lifetime.

*   Improves overall fitness, including muscular and cardiovascular.

*   Relieves stress and enhances creativity.

*   Reduces the appetite, burns calories, and is helpful in weight management.

Walking may appear to be a relatively boring activity; however, there are ways of creatively engaging employees in walking programs. Garazona (1989) described two such programs offered by the city of Seattle's municipal agency, METRO. "Flights to Fitness" is a stair climbing program conducted at the worksite to incorporate more exercise into the employee's workday. Employees participating in the program climb five flights of stairs daily for 25 weeks during the winter. Hidden along the staircase are coupons for a prize drawing. A similar program, "Walkablockalot" (WABAL), is a walking program designed as a scavenger hunt. "For example, participants may be asked if Larry Bird, the basketball player, would have enough head clearance to walk through the loading dock at 6th and Seneca" (p. 60). The incorporation of a scavenger hunt into the walking program promotes interest and challenge as employees seek answers to the list of clues. Prizes are awarded by random drawings and age-adjusted achievement. These programs are creative and were instituted at very low cost.

Appendix G provides two forms that may facilitate and track employee participation in a walking program. First, a short employee survey can be useful in identifying potential walkers as well as providing a pool of employees who may participate in the activity together. Second, walkers may record their participation in the walking program in order to document progress toward particular goals or simply to record overall involvement. Posting of weekly or monthly participation trends will provide feedback to gauge individual involvement. This form may also be useful for recording participation, which can then be utilized to recognize employees who have attained mileage award levels.

Corporate Sports Challenge

This community-wide special event challenges local companies to compete against each other in sports activities (Diani, 1989). The challenge is often sponsored by a YMCA or other non-profit organization, and the proceeds from the event are generally donated to a worthy community program. The primary objectives of the event are to promote healthier lifestyles, foster a more productive work environment, and enhance community participation and camaraderie through lifetime sports.

The sports challenge may include traditional and non-traditional sports such as golf, racquetball, darts, bowling, swimming, volleyball, horseshoes, a 10K race, and a 2K fun walk. Formats that allow for varying ability levels increase the potential for a successful event. The competition utilizes a point system for determining corporate champions who are then presented with awards or trophies.

Weight Loss Challenge

A weight loss challenge is a popular program with employees and one with documented success in helping individuals to lose weight. The weight loss program consists of a friendly competition between different companies or departments within a company challenging each other. The 12-week program is extremely easy to administer and consists of (1) a confidential initial weigh-in, (2) determination of each employee's weight loss goal (actual weight minus ideal weight, up to a maximum of 20 pounds), (3) a weekly weigh-in, (4) distribution of educational material on weight loss and nutrition, and (5) posting of weekly progress of the challenge. Employees contribute a minor fee to participate in the program.

A weight loss challenge program format was used in a research study between three local banks involving 200–300 employees, with the registration fee of $5 per person being awarded to the winning employees (Brownell, 1986). Results of the study found that fewer than 5% of the participants dropped out of the program. The average weight loss was 18.7 pounds for men and 11 pounds for women. A six month follow-up revealed that participants had maintained 80% of the weight loss. Similar results were found when departments within a company competed. In addition to the weight loss benefits to employees and the low cost of administration for companies, employees in the study also reported improved morale as a result of their involvement.

Smoking Cessation Program

Cigarette smoking has been identified as a major health risk for smokers, as well as nonsmokers who are subjected to second-hand smoke. The World Health Organization reported that smokers have much higher death rates than nonsmokers. Smokers are more likely than nonsmokers to die from heart disease, lung cancer, stroke, oral cancer, pulmonary disease, and ulcers. Nonsmokers who are subjected to cigarette smoke inhale about one-third the smoke that the individuals who are actively smoking do (Weiss, Fuhrmann, & Everly, 1985). According to Hoeger (1987), 75 – 90% of all smokers would like to quit.

Corporations have a stake in whether or not their employees smoke. Cigarette smoking has a direct effect on the health and medical costs absorbed by the corporation, and it affects employees' productivity in the workplace. Employees who have experienced health problems due to smoking have a higher absenteeism rate than nonsmokers. In addition, accidents are more likely to occur with smokers than nonsmokers (Weiss, Fuhrmann, Everly, 1985).

Programs that address smoking behaviors can focus on smoking cessation or smoking reduction. While there are obvious health advantages to reducing the number of cigarettes that are smoked, most programs focus on cessation. Smoking cessation programs can use a variety of interventions, all of which have their proponents. The most common smoking cessation techniques offered through employee services will be briefly reviewed below.

Education

All valid smoking cessation programs should begin with an educational component in which the person learns about the dangers of smoking as well as some of the common physical and emotional reactions to smoking cessation (Patton, et al., 1986). For some individuals, this education may be enough; others may require more structured follow-up.

Positive Reinforcement

Positive reinforcement techniques encourage the abstaining smokers to acknowledge repeatedly the positive consequences of their abstention; to reward themselves for their abstention, for example, by buying clothes with their saved cigarette money; and to substitute alternative behaviors during those times when they feel like smoking, such as going for a walk or doing some deep breathing. This technique seems to work effectively when used in conjunction with a support group of other individuals who are recovering smokers (Weiss, et al., 1985).

Stimulus Control

Stimulus control programs focus on the environmental cues that trigger the smoking response. Individuals are assisted in identifying through a self-monitoring sheet those situations that are associated with the desire to smoke. The smokers progressively restrict those situations in which they allow themselves to smoke. The smoker may use this as a reduction tool or a tapering off technique leading to total abstinence. This program is most effective with individuals whose primary reason for smoking is habit.

Stress Management

Stress management programs focus on the identification of primary life stressors and the acquisition of tools by the smoker to manage those stressors. Some smokers smoke most when they are anxious or feel unable to cope, and they view cigarette smoking as a crutch for getting through difficult times. Additionally, the cessation of smoking in itself creates stress. Stress management programs can perform a dual function in the cessation of smoking.

Combination Programs

Combination programs are the most effective for smoking cessation. Combination programs have reported a 40-70% abstention rate, while unidimensional programs have a 15-40% abstention rate after 6 months (Weiss, *et al.*, 1985). The most common combination programs include all of the above intervention techniques. It has also been recognized that the most effective way for smokers to quit is "cold turkey" rather than tapering off. In order to be effective, the program needs to focus on all stages of the cessation and maintenance process, including getting ready to quit, actually quitting, and the maintenance of abstinence.

Nutrition Program

There is a great deal of scientific support for the perspective that good nutrition is linked to good health. Proper nutrition provides individuals with the energy necessary to carry out their activities. In addition, proper nutrition provides the body with the raw materials for normal tissue growth, repair, and maintenance. Individuals today consume excessive amounts of fats, sugars and salts, often to the exclusion of more nutritious and healthy foods (Hoeger, 1987). Many individuals in society, including corporate employees, lack the basic information necessary to make informed nutritional choices.

According to Patton, *et al.* (1986), the goal of a nutrition program is to provide participants with information related to "food selection, preparation, and eating habits, and to teach them about the health problems arising from poor nutrition" (p. 158). Topics to be addressed can include reducing the intake of fats, sugars, and salt; the basic food groups and their contribution to health and well-being; how to prepare and cook foods in a manner that supports health; how to read nutritional labels on food products, and how to select nutritional foods.

Patton, *et al*. (1986), suggested various techniques for educating employees, including provision and labeling of cafeteria foods and vending machine choices, provision of information through flyers, demonstrations of cooking preparation, provision of a food reference library, and the sharing of healthy recipes through the company newsletter.

Perhaps the most effective way to promote nutritional change in employees is to include an individualized component in the program (Hoeger, 1987). Nutritional analysis assists individuals in rating their diets for nutritional value. Individuals track their diets for a three-day period by completing a diary of their intake of food and drink. Following the completion of this diary, the results may be discussed with a nutritionist or, minimally, compared to the Recommended Dietary Allowance outlined by the federal government. This encourages the participants in the program to examine their own diet specifically and make appropriate changes. This program requires the involvement of a specialist in nutrition in order for appropriate evaluation and dietary recommendations to be provided.

Retiree Club

Retiree clubs allow individuals who have retired to maintain contact and involvement with both the corporation and other retired workers. The corporation may provide resources to the club, such as space, financial backing, and speakers; however, the retirees should be directly involved in the governing of the club as well as in the planning and implementation of all activities (Hahler, 1987).

The activities of the Retiree Club should be based on a thorough needs assessment. Examples of activities that may be pursued by Retiree Club members include volunteer work in the community as well as in the sponsoring corporation; educational programs on topics of interest to the retirees; field trips; exercise and fitness programs; recreational activities, such as cards, bowling, or crafts; and retiree college programs.

Summary

This chapter has provided an overview and description of some of the most popular employee programs currently being offered through associations. There are also many traditional physical activity programs that are provided for employees through association clubs or leagues. A national survey of NESRA member employee associations found that the following physical activities were offered. For the 185 associations that completed the questionnaire, the percentage indicates the number of associations providing the activity (NESRA Market Survey, 1987).

softball	65%	bowling	51%
volleyball	50%	golf	49%
basketball	43%	fitness	35%
tennis	32%	jogging	28%
snow skiing	23%	fishing	17%
bicycling	15%	soccer	14%
football	10%	shooting	8%
racquetball	4%		

References

Brownell, K. D. (1986). Weight control in the workplace: The power of social and behavioral factors. In M. F. Cataldo and T. J. Coates, *Health and industry: A behavioral medicine perspective*. New York: Wiley.

Cato, D. (1988). Health awareness: Via a corporate health fair. *Employee Services Management*, 31(5), 8-12.

Cooper, K. (1983). *The aerobics program for total well being.* New York: Bantam.

Davis, K. & LeCompte, D. (1988). The business of aerobics. *Club Business*, 9(9), 48-54, 77-78.

Diani, F. E. (1989). Make it your business to run a corporate sports challenge. *Perspective*, 15(4), 48-4.

Garzona, C. (1989). How to get employees behind your program. *Personnel Administrator*, 34(10), 60-62.

Grumbine, E. (1989). Parenting fairs: Addressing work/family issues. *Employee Services Management*, 32(9), 8-10.

Hamman, C. (1989). Talkin' walkin.' *Employee Services Management*, 32(6), 33-35.

Hoeger, W. W. K. (1987). *The complete guide for the development & implementation of health promotion programs*. Englewood, CO: Morton.

Mazzeo, K. & Kisselle, J. (1987). *Aerobic dance: A way to fitness* (2nd edition). Englewood, CO: Morton.

Research USA, Inc. (1987). *NESRA Market Survey*. Westchester, IL: National Employee Services and Recreation Association.

Okerlund, K. (1984). Launching the corporate health fair. *Employee Services Management*, 27(1), 34-35.

Patton, R. W., Corry, J. M., Gettman, L. R. & Graf, J. S. (1986). *Implementing health/fitness programs*. Champaign, IL: Human Kinetics.

Robinson, M. G. (1985). Out of town workouts. *Employee Services Management*, 28(7), 29-30.

Rossman, J. R. (1989). *Recreation programming: Designing leisure experiences*. Champaign, IL: Sagamore Publishing.

Sweetgall, R. (1986). Walking: The road to fitness. *Employee Services Management*, 32(6), 15-18.

Walsh, S. Z. (1989). Service awards: Are you getting your money's worth? *Employee Services Management*, 32(6), 15-18.

Weiss, S. M., Fuhrmann, C. F. & Everly, G. S. Jr. (1985). The development of a smoking cessation program. In G. S. Everly, Jr. & R. H. L. Feldman, *Occupational health promotion*, New York: Wiley.

7

Program Implementation

There are many issues that are important to consider in the implementation of employee services and recreation programs. This chapter will discuss a few of the more salient ones, such as contracting for services, funding and pricing of programs, advertising and promotion, liability, and workers' compensation.

Contracting for Programs and Services

The first decision regarding program implementation is determining whether the activity will be provided by in-house staff or through outside experts. Contracting for the implementation of programs has become a popular method of satisfying the needs of both the association and the employees. Cooperative or contractual arrangements are often developed with hospitals, YMCA's, municipal recreation departments, private health and fitness facilities, health promotion companies, and universities. The support of contractual services provides the opportunity for additional program offerings to employees in a cost-effective manner. It is a method of increasing the effectiveness of existing staff resources without incurring the costs of hiring additional personnel. Contract services may take place at the worksite or at another location. Contract services are particularly desirable when the association does not have the expertise or facilities to implement needed programs.

The area of health promotion offers an association a realm of opportunities for contract services. Health promotion contractors usually provide some or all of the following: (1) health risk appraisals; (2) lifestyle change programs facilitated through classes, workshops, and special events; (3) modification of the work environment, such as changing the cafeteria menu; (4) evaluation of the program in measurable terms, such as reduced health care costs; and (5) incentives to motivate employees to participate in programs (Israel, 1989). Contractual arrangements should be made in consultation with the corporate lawyer.

Funding Employee Services and Recreation Programs

When employee services and recreation programs are a department within a corporation, services and programs may be funded directly from the company budget. Associations that are non-profit, separate entities may only receive partial subsidy from a company. For example, they may receive a salary line for a professional staff member and financial support for a limited number of specific programs. A recent NESRA survey (1988) determined the sources of revenue generation for employee associations and the percentage that each source contributed to their budgets. The company was the largest contributor, with 46%. It was followed by employee contributions, 17%; other (classes, photo processing), 14%; vending machines, 13%; employee store, 6%; discount sales, 4%.

However, regardless of the organizational structure of employee services and recreation programs, there is often inadequate corporate funding to meet all the needs and wants of employees. As a result, the generation of additional funds and the pricing of services and programs is of paramount importance. As indicated above, there are several methods that are available to employee associations for raising funds to augment company subsidies (Debats, 1981). Each of these financing methods will be identified and briefly described below.

Membership Dues

Employees can be charged a monthly or annual fee to become members of the employee association. The benefits of membership may include price differentials for members as opposed to non-members.

Vending Machine Profits

This method of supplementing corporate financing of employee services and recreation accrue to the association all profits from vending machines throughout the company.

User Fees

Employees are charged a fee for participation in services offered. This method suggests that those individuals who benefit from the program, the users, contribute to the cost of providing it. This is often an equitable way of sharing the cost of employee services and recreation programs between the company and the employee. One criteria useful for determining whether to assess user fees is if the program requires instructors from outside the company. The cost of instructors can be covered by an enrollment or registration fee.

Employee Store

Employee stores generate income while still providing convenience, savings, and unique items for employee purchase. Most "fair trade" items, those available in the community, are sold at a percentage markup over wholesale. There are two perspectives regarding the pricing of logo items. Logo items may be priced at a higher markup than "fair trade" items, generating greater financial returns, due to the uniqueness of the items and their unavailability elsewhere. A second perspective involves pricing logo merchandise at a lower markup than "fair trade" items in order to promote the company and its products.

Facility and Equipment Rental

Some employee services and recreation associations own their buildings and facilities and have the ability to rent rooms to the company for meetings, seminars, and workshops. In addition, recreational facilities or space may be rented to particular employee or community groups for special events. Further, retailers may contract with the association for space to sell their products, e.g., on-site Christmas tree sales and art and craft exhibits.

Equipment rental is also a method of generating revenue while saving employees money. This is particularly beneficial when equipment is either expensive or will be used only occasionally. In these instances, renting is more appealing than purchasing. Equipment rental by employee associations has included camping/outdoor equipment and athletic equipment (Cramer, 1985).

Newsletter Advertising

Businesses who provide company employees with discounts on services or merchandise are interested in advertising in the company newsletter. The advertising space sold to businesses encourages employees to take advantage of their discounts while providing funds for the association. When employee associations exist, the corporation itself may be required to pay a fee to advertise in the employees' newsletter.

Fund-raising Events

Fund-raising events can contribute significantly to the employee association's budget. Successful fund-raising events, such as the recycling of aluminum and paper and the sale of company equipment and product seconds and merchandise, have proven to be very profitable. Traditional fund-raisers (i.e., bake sales, employee craft sales) may also be worthwhile.

The referral category of fund raising provides reimbursement to the association from companies when employees make purchases. For example, contractual arrangements are made between the association and such retailers in the community as car dealerships, furniture companies, bulk food providers and jewelry stores. The association disseminates promotional materials to the employees for the companies or allows sales during lunch hours. If an employee makes a purchase from the retailer, the association receives a fee or percentage of sales in exchange for referral services.

Pricing Employee Services and Recreation Programs

There are several important factors to consider in the pricing of employee services and recreation programs. Figure 7.1

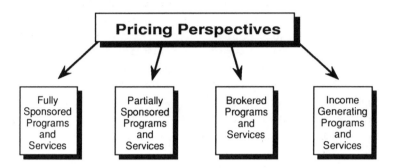

Figure 7.1
Pricing Model

provides an overview of four different pricing perspectives that apply to associations. A careful consideration of pricing perspectives is valuable, philosophically, in that it allows the programmer to determine the option that is most congruent with the goals of the company and the employee association.

Fully Sponsored Programs and Services

Fully sponsored Programs and Services are those that provide the benefits most often desired by the company and most in accordance with its own philosophy. The company would have a strong and vested interest in ensuring that every employee has the opportunity to take advantage of and participate in these programs. As a result, these programs and services are completely funded by the company. A company-wide health fair is a good example of a program that often is fully sponsored because of the benefit derived to the corporation and employees.

Partially Sponsored Programs and Services

Partially-sponsored Programs and Services constitute programmatic offerings that support the goals and emphasis of both the association and the company, but may be targeted to smaller groups of employees. In this case, the association and the company provide a percentage of the funding, and employees who participate are required to contribute to the cost of the program through user fees. Partial sponsoring by the association would cover the majority of the program expenses. This would ensure that employees could receive the program with only a small charge, generally below the cost of similar programs in the community. Sports leagues are usually partially sponsored by the company.

Brokered Programs and Services

Brokered Programs and Services are those activities of the association that are conducted on behalf of the employees and in which there is no company cost to the employee and no financial gain for the association. Brokered programs and services include the dissemination of educational information and referral to community service providers.

Income-generating Programs and Services

Income-generating Programs and Services are those activities of the association that, while benefiting employees, are not directly attributable to long-term employee or company goals. The generation of income, as previously discussed, is vital to the ability of the association to fully or partially sponsor or fund services and programs. The employee store and photo processing are common methods of generating income.

Both partially sponsored and income-generating programs and services provide associations with the opportunity to determine the price or level of employee financial contribution for activities or services. There are three different types of pricing strategies appropriate for employee associations, including (1) cost-oriented pricing, (2) demand-oriented pricing, and (3) competition-oriented pricing (Kotler and Andreasen, 1987).

Cost-oriented pricing refers to setting prices largely on the basis of costs. The most popular cost-oriented pricing method is break-even analysis. In order to determine a price using this cost-oriented method, all fixed and variable costs must be identified. Fixed costs are those that do not vary (e.g., building insurance, staff salaries, equipment). Variable costs include those that change depending upon the number of employees who participate in the program. Variable costs would include such things as program materials, the number of instructors, awards, and T-shirts. Once the costs have been determined, the association director can determine the expense of running the program or providing the service. If a particular program or service is intended to generate income for a department or association, monies obtained through the program must be above the break-even point.

One method of cost-oriented pricing that is used in retail businesses is markup pricing. With markup pricing, a fixed percentage is added to the cost of each item. Markup pricing would most likely occur in the association's employee store.

The use of cost-oriented pricing allows for flexibility in determining the fixed costs to include in the calculation. For example, the cost of program space may be included as a fixed cost and contribute to the final price. However, fixed costs such as building space may be eliminated from the price determination with the justification that the company already is supporting this cost. Fairness should be the overriding factor in determining which fixed costs to include in the price calculation.

Demand-oriented pricing examines the demand for the program or service, rather than the actual cost, to determine the price. In this method, estimates are made regarding the value employees perceive in the program or service, and prices are set accordingly. The price is a direct reflection of the program's perceived value to the employee. In other words, the price is a result of the employees' willingness to pay. This strategy allows for the opportunity to develop price differentials for association members and non-members. Further, it is possible to heighten demand for the program or service through increasing its perceived value, resulting in a higher price.

Competition-oriented pricing basically means determining prices on the basis of what others in the community are charging. The choices are to charge the same, higher, or lower prices than the competition. This is a popular method in situations where it is difficult to measure costs and when it is important to represent prices as similar to those charged in the community. Ascertaining the price of programs and services in the community is an easy undertaking, with a phone call or program brochures providing this information.

Pricing is an important task of the employee services and recreation manager. Receiving subsidization of employee programs and services provides an opportunity to increase the variety of activities offered through the association while affording employees the opportunity to participate at reduced rates. Further, income generated from employee services, such as employee stores, supports additional programs that would not have been possible. Cost-oriented pricing is the fairest method of determining fees and charges.

Advertising and Promotion

Advertising and promotion are the tools utilized to communicate to employees the opportunities for involvement in the association's programs and services. An important component of advertising is the creation of the message, which should clearly focus on the needs of employees and the benefits available through participation in association activities. Often messages can be linked to national themes, such as nutrition month or employee health and fitness day, and include several communication efforts to stimulate employee interest and participation. For example, Rawson (1987) reported on a lifestyle seminar that was titled "Turn Over A New Leaf On Life." Each employee received a leaf on his or her desk one week before the seminar. Underneath the leaf was a note that read "A Sign Of Things To Come On May 21st."

There are a variety of low-cost methods available in the corporate setting to advertise and promote programs. Some of these include

flyers   bulletin boards
electronic message boards   buttons and balloons

printed messages on paychecks   posters
interoffice mail   easel signs
cafeteria placemats and tray liners   information packets
brochures and handouts   stickers and mementos
company newsletters   paycheck stubs

Company Newsletter

A company newsletter is an excellent vehicle for communicating with employees regarding the programs and services offered through the association. Company newsletters are read by most employees and can provide a wealth of information. There are several goals for a company newsletter (Yendell, 1985).

Some of these include

*   To inform employees regarding the activities of the company, in terms of policies, business trends, achievements, and future prospects.

*   To build employees' pride and interest in their work through highlighting the value of employee contributions.

*   To promote corporate culture and employee loyalty.

*   To increase efficiency by promoting employee safety, health, and fitness; by reducing waste, absenteeism, and tardiness and by incorporating ideas and changes through employee involvement.

*   To boost morale by featuring employees on the job and at home and by recognizing the accomplishments of employees and their family members.

An employee newsletter is an invaluable resource for communicating to employees news about the events and activities of the association while providing information of value to the company and employees alike.

Liability

Liability is a significant concern for any organization providing recreation areas, facilities, and programs. There has been an increase in the number of liability lawsuits filed in this country. In fact, a recent survey revealed that 84% of respondents were more likely to file a personal injury suit than in the past (Kittrell, 1987). It is the responsibility of the company and association to ensure the safety and protection of both participants and staff. While safe programs, services and facilities protect employees from injury, they also forestall the possibility of costly litigation.

Tort liability is a civil wrong in which one party injures another. In the great majority of recreational injury cases, the issue of liability has involved the tort of negligence (Kozlowski, 1988). A company may be negligent for an employee's injury if the injury results from a failure to supervise properly an activity or event, maintain a safe playing surface, or distribute safe and proper equipment. Also, if an employee was injured as a result of participating in an activity, but was unaware of the potential risks for injury or impaired health, the company may be liable (Grumbine, 1989).

In most recreational injury liability cases, there is a failure on the part of the provider to act reasonably under the circumstances (Kozlowski, 1988). That is, areas, facilities, and programs were challenged as being unsafe. One step toward reducing liability is to provide reasonable care. Kaizer (1987) has provided a set of principles that is prudent and offers reasonable care to participants and staff while reducing the potential for liability. These guidelines are broken down into those for supervisors and activity instructors.

General Supervisory Obligations

1. Where an activity or area involves a high risk of serious injury, specific supervision is required.

2. Safety and operational rules for areas, facilities, and programs must be developed, posted, and enforced.

3.   Participants must be protected from the acts of rowdyism, boisterous conduct, fighting, and dangerous activity of others.

4.   Supervisors should remain at their supervisory posts and leave only in emergency circumstances.

5.   Participants should be warned of any hidden dangers present in the conduct of programs or in the maintenance of areas.

6.   Facilities that present a high risk of injury should be locked and equipment made inaccessible when unsupervised use could reasonably be expected to cause injury.

7.   Facilities and equipment should be regularly inspected and defects corrected or participants warned of their existence.

Conduct of Programs Involving Activity Instruction

1.   Prepare instructional plans indicating program goals, performance measures, and testing procedures, and adhere to this plan in conducting the program.

2.   Provide appropriate, properly designed, and well maintained protective and safety equipment.

3.   Inspect all program equipment for defects, and remove defective   equipment from use.   Maintenance records should be established according to manufacturers' guidelines and practices.

4.   Group participants in contact sports according to age, maturity, weight, height, and motor skill.

5.   Evaluate participants' physical conditioning and skill level prior to their undertaking high risk recreational activities.

6.   Warn participants of the unique and particular risks of an activity. Never assume that participants know and under-

stand all of the risks that may result in injury from participation.

7.   Develop written policies that specify emergency procedures for the provision of proper medical assistance for injuries.

8.   Institute, practice, and follow emergency procedures for transporting injured persons to appropriate medical facilities.

Adapted from Kaiser 1986, pp. 190-191.

The assumption of risk by the participant has been one of the widely used defenses to the charge of negligence. The assumption of risk indicates that the employee is fully aware of and appreciates the risks inherent in participating in the activity. Further, the employee carefully and reasonably agrees to assume whatever risks are involved (Berry & Wong, 1986). It is also important that the employee voluntarily participates in the activity.

Waivers

Waivers are used to release a program sponsor from potential liability and negligence by having employees assume the risk of participating. There are three criteria for designing a waiver:

1.   "It must be explicitly worded.

2.   "If there are rules that must be followed, they should be listed in the agreement or on the reverse side of the form. If they are not included, wording should be included indicating that the participant has received the rules, has read and understands them, and will abide by them.

3.   "The possible dangers inherent in the activities must be spelled out in detail along with the consequences of possible accidents so the participant can appreciate the risks and

their possible consequences. The participant must sign a statement expressly assuming the risks of participation" (Peterson, 1987, pp. 15-16).

Waivers indicate that the injured participant has as-sumed the risks of the activity and gives up the right to sue for damages incurred. Waivers may provide protection to the association from lawsuits when the waiver is properly admin-istered and clearly defines the dangers inherent in the activity, and the participant voluntarily signs the release (Brown, 1989). Developing a participant waiver requires the consultation of an attorney in order to ensure adherence to state law and the validity of the release. A sample waiver and accident report form are provided in Appendix H.

Workers' Compensation

Workers' compensation has become an avenue employ-ees are utilizing to receive remuneration for injuries that result from participation in recreation programs. Employers are re-quired to carry workers' compensation, which provides benefits and medical care to employees for injuries that are a result of their employment. Each state has its own workers' compensation legislation and system (Clement, 1988). This insurance system provides benefits that are financed by employer-paid premiums. The amount of the premium is determined by the safety record of the industry and the individual employer (Heneman, Schwab, Fossum & Dyer, 1989).

Workers' compensation ensures that every employee is protected under the system without regard to fault. The intent is to provide full medical treatment and disability benefits until the employee can return to work. The coverage extends to employee injuries that arise out of, and occur during, the course of employ-ment (Vanner, 1988). An injured employee does not have to prove negligence on the part of the employer — only that he or she suffered a work-related injury. In return, the employee gives up the right to sue for full damages and cannot be found guilty of contributory negligence or assumption of risk (Baley and Matthews, 1989).

The primary issue in employee services and recreation has been whether involvement in programs falls within the course of employment. The issue of what constitutes a work-related injury is decided by state courts. Specifically, the courts focus on the extent of company involvement in the provision of the activity and the extent to which the company benefited from the employee's participation. Company involvement includes such factors as its financial support of the program, required or expected attendance of employees, the delivery of official speeches, and the presentation of awards or gifts at the event. The issue of company benefits spans those previously discussed in Chapter 2 and revolves around the degree to which the company benefited from the employee's involvement in the program. (Schultz, 1985).

Grumbine (1989) reported the case of Vaccaro vs. Sperry Rand Corporation. In this case, an employee suffered a heart attack while jogging on the employer's property. Since jogging was permitted and employees were provided with an athletic facility, the court ruled that the death was work-related. Each state's workers' compensation laws are different, and employee services and recreation managers should be aware of their laws. For example, Illinois, Maine and California have proclaimed that injuries resulting from voluntary involvement in company sponsored recreation programs are not necessarily covered by workers' compensation. Other states are judging claims on a case-by-case basis.

Summary

The implementation of programs and services requires careful attention to details in order to ensure success. This chapter has discussed contracting for programs and services, pricing, advertising, promotion, and the area of employee safety. There are a myriad of additional details to be considered and tasks to be performed by a variety of association staff. It is often useful to organize these tasks and details through the use of a flow chart or checklist. This facilitates the determination of relevant implementation tasks and the assignment of particular responsibilities to staff. A sample programmer's checklist is provided in Appendix I.

References

Baley, J.A. & Matthews, D.L. (1989). *Law and liability in athletics, physical education andrecreation* (2nd edition). Dubuque, I. C. Brown.

Berry R. C. & Wong, G. M. (1986). *Law and business of the sports industries* (Vol. II). Dover, MA: Auburn House.

Brown, S. C. (1989). The impact of case law on liability waivers. *Journal of Sport Management*, 3(2), 5-14.

Clement, A. (1988). *Law in sport and physical activity*. Indianapolis, IN: Benchmark.

Debats, K. (1981). Industrial recreation programs: A new look at an old benefit. *Personnel Journal*, August, 620-627.

Grumbine, E. D. (1989). Program liability: Safeguarding your company-sponsored activities. *Employee Services Management*, 32(8), 12-14.

Henemen, H. G., Schwab, D. P., Fossum, J. A. & Dyer, L. D. (1989). *Personnel/human resource management* (4th edition). Homewood, IL: Irwin.

Israel, D. (1989). Contracting for fitness. *Employee Services Management*, 32(9), 24-26.

Kaiser, R. A. (1986). *Liability and law in recreation, parks and sports*. Englewood Cliffs, NJ: Prentice-Hall.

Kittrell, A. (1987). Public sees rise in number and size of lawsuits: Study. *Business Insurance* , p. 3.

Kotler, P. & Andreasen, A. R. (1987). *Strategic marketing for nonprofit organizations*, (3rd edition). Englewood cliffs, NJ: Prentice-Hall.

Kozlowski, J. C. (1988). A common sense view of liability. *Parks and Recreation*, 23(9), 56-59.

Peterson, J. A. (1987). *Risk management for park, recreation and leisure services*. Champaign, IL: Management Learning Laboratories.

Rawson, A. (1987).Wellness: Make it happen through effective communications. In S. H. Klarreich (ed.) *Health and fitness in the workplace*. New York: Praeger.

Schultz, J. H. (1985). Employee recreation and fitness programs and worker's compensation: A continuing saga. *Employee Services Management*, 28(8), 19-22.

Survey results: Employee recreation associations. *Employee Services Management*, 31(10), 5.

Vanner, B. S. (1988). Cut beneath the abuse of worker's compensation. *Personnel Journal*, 67(4), 30-32.

Yendell, P. (1985). Your company newsletter—how to make it write. *Employee Services Management*, 28(4), 20-25.

8

The Evaluation of Programs and Services

The evaluation of programs and services is the final component of programming. Evaluation is a process through which a manager gathers information on the merit or worth of a program or service. The overall goal of evaluation is to improve the quality of programs and services that are provided to employees. As illustrated in the program planning model (Figure 1.1, Chapter 1), program evaluation is guided by the mission of employee services and recreation. For example, the questions posed and data collected through the evaluation effort will focus primarily on information related to the intended purposes of the corporation in sponsoring an employee association. One type of evaluation, the needs assessment, was previously described in Chapter 3. This chapter will provide an introduction and perspective on additional program evaluation techniques. The evaluation procedures to be discussed are practical in nature and applicable in the corporate setting.

Purpose of Evaluation

The two principle purposes of evaluation are program management and accountability. First, evaluation supports the program management function by providing the manager with feedback on the strengths and weaknesses of the program as it is currently being conducted. Evaluation techniques may be used to gather the information necessary for a manager to make an informed decision regarding program provision, modification, or termination. Evaluation can focus on a number of different issues, such as the determination of goal attainment, utilization of resources, examination of implementation, delivery of services, and the measurement of program/service outcomes (Madaus, Stufflebeam, & Scriven, 1983).

Second, program evaluation may be used to collect data to demonstrate program accountability to the corporation and/or its employees. There is an increased demand from funding sources, as well as consumers, that service providers be responsible for both the effectiveness and the efficiency of those services provided. Objective data is used to demonstrate to others the benefits associated with the program as well as the appropriate utilization of resources. According to Edington, Edington, & Yen (1988), few employee services managers are currently required to justify programs and services. However, corporations are increasingly interested in the return they obtain from their financial investment in employee services and recreation programs. Without program evaluation, which provides accountability information, employee services and recreation departments are likely to experience diminished funding.

Process Evaluation

Once a needs assessment has been conducted and the program has been organized, developed, and implemented, the employee services manager can begin a process evaluation. Process evaluation is concerned with assessing the program itself, its activities, the population it serves, and how it functions (Posavac & Carey, 1989). The purpose is to determine why the program succeeded or failed and to indicate any required revisions. In addition, a process evaluation describes what happened as the program progressed from the beginning to its conclusion (Windsor, Baranowski, Clark & Cutter, 1984). This is a very common type of evaluation and should be a basic component of any evaluation system.

There are several specific uses of a process evaluation that involve monitoring the program while it is being implemented and documenting the program at its conclusion (King, Morris & Fitz-Gibbon, 1987). First, monitoring a program as it is implemented recognizes that programs should be changed or adjusted as they are being conducted in order to meet effectively the current needs of the participants and the goals of the program. Implementation monitoring allows the manager to assist staff in identifying particular aspects of a program that may not be working, determine appropriate modifications, or use alternative strategies. In addition, program staff may not be following the program plan and a process evaluation may be useful in bringing this to the manager's attention. The manager may then redirect staff efforts in order to promote a successful program.

Monitoring the implementation of a program also ensures that changes made in the program plan are documented. It is often difficult for staff to remember all the modifications and details in the plan at the conclusion of a program. As a result of an ongoing process evaluation, an accurate description can be created to serve as the basis for future programming efforts. In addition, at the conclusion of a program, a debriefing meeting with all program staff is scheduled. This meeting affords the opportunity to discuss fully the program's implementation and to record suggestions for changes in future events.

Second, the documentation of the program through a process evaluation provides accountability information on how money allocated to the program was spent. It ensures that staff justify expenditures according to the program plan. In addition, a comparison of the projected and actual costs of the program should be determined at the conclusion of the program. This documents the extent to which the association or corporation financed the event and the costs associated per participant. Further, a comparison of costs provides information for future pricing decisions. Two sample final program cost evaluation report forms are provided in Appendix J.

King, *et al.* (1987), have provided a list of 300 questions that can be answered through a process evaluation. The following are some examples:

*   Is the program attracting a sufficient number of participants?

*   Did the program attract the targeted participants?

*   Are the qualifications of the program staff appropriate?

*   Was the program implemented as designed?

*   Were the facilities, equipment, and supplies adequate?

*   Is the environment safe for participants and staff?

*   Is the program delivered at an appropriate level (e.g., beginner)?

*   Was the length of the program appropriate?

There are three methods of collecting data for process evaluations. First, data can be obtained from corporate and program records. The personnel department collects data in areas such as absenteeism, sick days, and job satisfaction. In addition, program registration forms and instructor attendance sheets can be utilized to answer certain process questions. However, program records need to be designed to meet the specific requirements of the process evaluation. Program records that are directly designed to address process questions will facilitate the evaluation.

Second, information for process evaluations can be collected by observing the program while it is being implemented. This is often a time-consuming process, and it requires attention to detail in order for the information to be useful. However, it is the most effective mechanism for defining exactly what is occurring in the program and whether the program plan is being implemented as designed.

Finally, staff and participants can complete questionnaires that address key evaluation issues. It is important to gather information related to the experiences and perceptions of the leaders and participants. The reliance on information from an objective observer may not capture the experience and satisfaction of those directly involved. Sample participant program evaluation forms are provided in Appendix L.

An example of process evaluation, identified by Parkinson and Associates (1982) as the inventory approach, requires that data be collected regularly at meaningful intervals. This information allows for the description of the program's efforts over a period of time. It is often useful to depict inventory process evaluation data in graphical form to describe particular evaluation issues. In order to demonstrate a graph using the inventory approach, the following data was created for illustrative purposes only. Figure 8.1 portrays the number of employees who decreased their smoking after being involved in a smoking cessation program.

Figure 8.1
Smoking Cessation Program

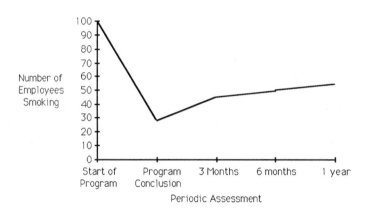

It is important to recognize that this type of information is simply describing what happened to participants. It does not determine that the smoking cessation program caused a reduction in smoking behavior. This type of inference requires more sophisticated evaluation procedures.

A second illustration of the inventory approach is depicted in Figure 8.2. In this graph, employee absenteeism is charted prior to and after the implementation of a childcare program.

Figure 8.2
Childcare and Employee Absenteeism

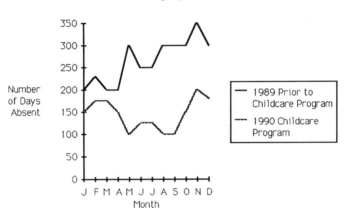

This graph requires the use of company records, which may be difficult to obtain due to employee confidentiality regulations. However, when the information is available, the evaluation often can be more meaningful. The use of graphs such as these provide employee services managers with an excellent method of describing program efforts. Graphs can be utilized in annual reports of the association and should be provided to management to gain support.

Evaluation of Participant Satisfaction

Assessing participant satisfaction is an evaluation technique used to determine participant outcomes from involvement in recreation programs (Rossman, 1982; 1983; 1989). This type of evaluation technique emanates from a theoretical basis and has been field tested with employees involved in association programs. The employees in Rossman's study participated in 15 different programs offered by the Johnson's Wax Employee Services and Recreation Association and completed a self-report participant satisfaction questionnaire.

The results of this field testing indicated that satisfaction with participation in a particular program is represented by scores in ten different domains. These domains include achievement, physical fitness, social enjoyment, family escape, environment, risk, family togetherness, relaxation, fun, and autonomy. Each domain contains several satisfaction statements that can be selected by the evaluator to judge specific programs. Additional items can be incorporated to evaluate satisfaction with other aspects of the program that are not included in these ten domains (e.g., price, scheduling). A complete set of the satisfaction questionnaire items and scoring procedures can be found in Rossman (1989).

Participant-reported satisfaction with programs can play an important role in the evaluation process. First, satisfaction data can be useful to the program manager in determining whether program goals and objectives are being accomplished. That is, if the goal is to promote family togetherness, high satisfaction with this domain would be an indicator of attaining this goal. Second, a program manager may use the evaluation data to determine strong and weak programs. The information may be used to discontinue or modify aspects of those programs found to be low in satisfaction by the participants. Third, program formats can be investigated to determine which satisfactions are facilitated through the use of particular program structures. For example, a club in which retirees determine their own travel plans, hold their own meetings, and do their own fund-raising may be perceived as more satisfying than a leader-directed travel group.

Efficiency Evaluation

Efficiency evaluation is concerned with the issue of cost. There are two basic types of efficiency evaluation: cost-benefit and cost-effectiveness. Each of these evaluations begins with an examination of fixed and variable program costs. In cost-benefit analysis, the costs of the program are evaluated in terms of the benefits accrued to employees and the corporation as a result of the program or service. The difficulty with this evaluation method lies in determining the financial value of intangible benefits in order to make comparisons. For example, what dollar amount would accrue to the company from individuals participating in an employee walking program or a computer club? This example suggests that it is extremely difficult, if not impossible, to compare costs and benefits in this manner.

The employee store is one area in which an association can conduct a modification of the cost-benefit analysis. One of the main purposes of the employee store is to save employees money on their purchases. It is common for associations to calculate the savings that employees receive from purchasing items at the employee store as compared to retail outlets. Figure 8.3 illustrates employee savings by year. (This example is fictitious.) Included in this calculation are the actual costs of operating the employee store. As a result, this graph indicates the dollar value benefits to employees after the operational costs of the employee store are deducted.

The second type of efficiency evaluation, cost-effectiveness, determines the best program or service alternative for the

Figure 8.3
Employee Savings from Company Store

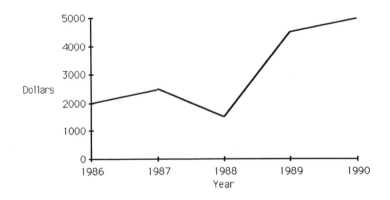

cost involved. Essentially, cost-effectiveness examines whether one program achieves a better level of success than others costing the same or less to administer (Posavac & Carey, 1989). For example, an evaluation could be conducted to compare an in-house wellness program with one that is provided by outside contractors. If the results indicate that the in-house program costs the same, but the outcomes attained are higher than the outside consultants, it would indicate that the in-house program was more cost-effective. In addition, it is important to determine whether program costs are reasonable even when the desired benefits are achieved. This is a very common sense approach to obtaining the best programs and services for the funds expended and at a cost that is not prohibitive.

Summary

This chapter has provided an introduction to the evaluation of employee programs and services. While the techniques illustrated are not comprehensive in nature, they do provide a basis for gathering relevant data on which to base decisions. The mission of employee services and recreation determines what type of information should be collected and the types of evaluation methods required. It is important to note that several evaluation techniques should be utilized to evaluate programs and services. This ensures that the evaluation is balanced and integrates a variety of perspectives. The manager of employee services may benefit from taking advantage of in-house corporate personnel, such as data analysts, to supplement the expertise of program staff in the evaluation process.

References

Edington, D. W., Edington, M. & Yen, L. (1988). The formula for proving your program's worth. *Employee Services Management*, 31(10), 12-13, 16-17.

King, J. A., Morris, L. L. & Fitz-Gibbon, C. T. (1987). *How to assess program implementation*. Beverly Hills, CA: Sage.

Madaus, G. F., Stufflebeam, D. L. & Scriven, M. S. (1983). Program evaluation: A historical overview. In G. F. Madaus, D. L. Stufflebeam & M. S. Scriven (eds.) *Evaluation models: Viewpoints of educational and human services evaluation*. Boston, MA: Kluwer-Nijhoff.

Parkinson, R. B. & Associates (1982). *Managing health promotion in the workplace: Guidelines for implementation and evaluation*. Palo Alto, CA: Mayfield.

Posavac, E. J. & Carey, R. G. (1989). *Program evaluation: Methods and case studies* (3rd edition). Englewood Cliffs, NJ: Prentice-Hall.

Rossman, J. R. (1982) Evaluate programs by measuring participant satisfactions. *Parks & Recreation*, 33-35.

Rossman, J. R. (1983). Participant satisfaction with employee recreation. *Journal of Physical Education, Recreation and Dance*. 54(8), 60-62.

Rossman, J. R. (1989). *Recreation programming: Designing leisure experiences*. Champaign, IL: Sagamore.

Windsor, R. A., Baranowski, T., Clark, N. & Cutter, G. (1984). *Evaluation of health promotion and education programs*. Palo Alto, CA: Mayfield.

9

Shaping The Future

There are several challenges facing society that have direct implications for the employee services and recreation manager. In concluding this book, an attempt will be made to identify some of the pertinent issues that will affect the provision of employee and recreation programs in the near future. Taking a proactive stance regarding these challenges and issues is essential. Attempting to develop programs and services that are responsive to these issues allows the employee services and recreation manager to contribute to the shaping of the future. This perspective will enhance the importance of the contribution of employee services and recreation programs to the employee and to the corporation.

Factors Affecting the Future

One significant factor affecting the future is the changing composition of society and its resultant impact on the workforce and corporations. The aging of society will have major implications for employee services and recreation. In particular, it is estimated that by the year 2000, the median age of workers will be 39, while the number of younger workers entering the labor pool will decline by 8%. In addition, 25 million people will enter the workforce between 1989 and 2000. Of this group of potential employees, approximately 85% will be women and minorities, including, African-Americans, Hispanics, Asians, Native Americans and Pacific islanders. Only 15% will be white males (Solomon, 1989). Corporations will face particular challenges related to this multicultural workforce.

In addition, due to already occurring shortages of workers, employers will be hiring individuals who have not previously been mainstreamed into the workforce. People with disabilities finally will receive the attention from employers that they deserve, and their rate of hire by corporations will increase. Corporations also will attempt to entice older workers back into the workplace to offset the decline of available employees. Further, ex-offenders will be incorporated into the workforce in greater numbers (Wagel, 1990). These changes will alter the future of corporations while adding to the challenges of employee services and recreation.

The aging of society will not only impact the workplace with regard to older employees, but will also confront employees who are caring for older relatives. A recent survey indicated that the requirements of eldercare affect employee productivity, absenteeism, turnover, and morale (Magus, 1988). As a result, eldercare has been described as the emerging employee benefit (Azarnoff, 1988).

Another work and family issue becoming more prevalent is childcare. The effect of increasing numbers of women entering the workforce has had the impact of altering corporate policies to accommodate the needs of women. Parental leave, referral services for childcare, subsidized childcare, on-site childcare facilities, and sick childcare options are some of the ways corporations are responding to women in the workforce (Grumbine, 1989).

Flextime is emerging as one response to the needs of employees that allows them to balance the demands and obligations of work and family. Under the most common flextime arrangement, employees must be present at the worksite during core hours, for example, between 9 a.m. and 11 a.m. and between 1 p.m. and 3 p.m, but they can determine their own starting and quitting times. This system assists in the recruitment of employees who otherwise would be unable to work full-time. There has been some evidence that flextime reduces absenteeism, the use of leave time, and overtime (Heneman, Schwab, Fossum & Dyer, 1989). In addition, corporations are increasing their implementation of work-at-home options. Sophisticated technology, such as personal computers, electronic mail, and fax machines has fostered the opportunity to work at home, which has been referred to as flexplace. It is relatively easy for employees to communicate with the office and carry out their responsibilities at home. The advantages for the corporations include reduced overhead, increased productivity, and company loyalty (Grumbine, 1989).

According to a 1985 survey of employee benefits by the U.S. Chamber of Commerce, companies in the U.S. spent $2,560 per employee for health care (Sloan & Gruman, 1988). Health care costs are increasing at 12% to 15% each year (Everly, 1985). It is estimated that 60% of health care costs are the result of unhealthy lifestyle habits and poor stress management (Adams, 1988). It has been suggested that in the future, health promotion programs no longer will be seen as merely fringe benefits, but will be an acknowledged part of the work experience. Indeed, health promotion programs may become synonymous with productivity, performance, and organizations that care about their employees (Matteson and Ivancevich, 1988).

Addressing the Future

Addressing future changes in society and the workforce will require attempting to understand and respond to the needs of corporations and employees. Some suggestions for employee services and recreation managers have been identified by Tindell (1988) and include the following:

*   Promote health, wellness, and recreation opportunities provided directly through associations or through access to private health and fitness clubs.

*   Include mid-day opportunities for exercise breaks.

*   Enhance feelings of belonging for employees who wish to work at home, and provide these individuals with information about recreation and fitness programs in close proximity to their homes.

*   Provide programs and opportunities particularly geared to the older worker, including health benefits, appropriate fitness programs and seminars on pre-retirement and financial planning issues. Grumbine (1989) also suggests

that older workers have different motivations, including making a contribution to their community. Involvement in community service projects and volunteering in association programs may meet their needs.

*   Provide lifestyle management programs.

*   Respond to the needs of minority workers.   Consider recreation opportunities that are particularly meaningful to different cultural groups. These programs should take into account the distinct value systems, work styles, and leisure ethics of specific cultures. In addition, programs should attempt to create understanding between these groups of people. For example, organizing an international food day, where employees bring dishes that reflect their ethnic backgrounds would facilitate communication and understanding between employees (Grumbine, 1989). Further, recognizing ethnic holidays and festivals, such as Chinese New Year and Chanukah, would also be meaningful to particular groups of employees.

*   Address the needs of professional couples with families. The need for childcare and programs geared around families and lifestyles will be crucial.

Conclusion

The perspective of this book has been to enhance the provision of programs and services that are responsive to the needs of employees while also addressing the concerns of the corporation and management. It is a delicate balancing act for employee services and recreation departments to incorporate the perspectives of employees, management, and professional staff in their delivery of programs and services. In order to be responsive to these groups, associations must conduct needs assessments annually and utilize this information as the basis for program development. Once programs have been identified, organized, developed, and implemented, evaluation procedures should be utilized to gain an understanding of the contribution or worth of the program for employees and the corporation. This information directly impacts the provision of future programs and services.

Responding to the future is certainly a challenge for any organization. Associations and Employee Services and Recreation Departments can position themselves for future prosperity by providing meaningful programs and services to employees and documenting the program outcomes for management. The future looks bright for employee services and recreation, and the challenge awaits.

References

Azarnoff, R. S. (1988). Can employees carry the eldercare burden? *Personnel Journal*, 67(9), 60-65.

Grumbine, E. (1989). Adjusting to a varied workforce. *Employee Services Management*, 32(10), 13-16.

Henemen, H. G., Schwab, D. P., Fossum, J. A. & Dyer, L. D. (1989). *Personnel/human resource management* (4th edition). Homewood, IL: Irwin.

Solomon, C. M. (1989). The corporate response to workforce diversity. *Personnel Journal*, 68(8), 43-53.

Tindell, J. P. (1988). Managers as futurists: Addressing changing employee needs. *Employee Services Management*, 31(4), 34-37.

Appendix A
Sample Needs Assessment

EMPLOYEES' ASSOCIATION

San Diego Gas & Electric • P.O. Box 1831 • San Diego, California 92112

Dear Member:

The SDG&E Employees' Association wants to get to know you a little better. We want to know what you like and what you don't like so we can provide you with the kinds of events and services that YOU WANT.

So, we asked Consumer Research to design a questionnaire that would help us learn more about you. We are going to use this information to help plan and organize better activities, to determine which discount tickets you want and to assess how well we communicate with our members. That's why it's important for all members to participate in this study.

We would like you to take a couple of minutes and answer the questions on the attached questionnaire. When you are done, simply place your completed questionnaire in the interoffice mail. We have included the return address on the questionnaire so you don't need to use an interoffice envelope. Consumer Research will receive your completed questionnaire and it will be kept strictly confidential.

Remember, this is your opportunity to help make the SDG&E Employees' Association the kind of organization that you want. Take the time to tell us what you want.

Sincerely,

Maria Higgins   Mark Ward
President   Vice President

P.S. We need your help. Would you please return your completed questionnaire by September 9.

SDG&E Employees' Association Survey for Members

Awareness and Level of Interest

The SDG&E Employees' Association would like to find out if members are aware of the many special events and discount tickets that the association offers and determine which special events and tickets you might be likely to use *within the next 12 months*. Please answer questions 1 and 2 below by circling one number for each question and for each of the special events or discount tickets on the chart below.

1. Were you aware that the SDG&E Employees' Association offered the following services?

2. How likely do you think you would be to use the service *within the next 12 months*?

	Question 1 Aware offered?		Question 2 How likely would you be to purchase?		
Discount tickets	Was aware	Was not aware	Very	Not very	Not sure
Movie theatres	1	2	1	2	3
Padres	1	2	1	2	3
SD Sockers	1	2	1	2	3
Circus	1	2	1	2	3
Ice Capades	1	2	1	2	3
SDSU Aztecs	1	2	1	2	3
Del Mar Fair	1	2	1	2	3
Air Shows	1	2	1	2	3
See's Candy	1	2	1	2	3

Discount tickets to amusment parks	Question 1 Aware offered?		Question 2 How likely would you be to purchase?		
	Was aware	Was not aware	Very	Not very	Not sure
Sea World	1	2	1	2	3
Disneyland	1	2	1	2	3
Knotts Berry Farm	1	2	1	2	3
Magic Mountain	1	2	1	2	3
Zoo	1	2	1	2	3
Wild Animal Park	1	2	1	2	3
Queen Mary	1	2	1	2	3
Family Fun Center	1	2	1	2	3
Universal Studios	1	2	1	2	3

Group Trips	Question 1 Aware offered?		Question 2 How likely would you be to purchase?		
	Was aware	Was not aware	Very	Not very	Not sure
Las Vegas	1	2	1	2	3
Laughlin	1	2	1	2	3
Palm Springs	1	2	1	2	3
Canoeing	1	2	1	2	3
Snow Skiing	1	2	1	2	3
Garment District	1	2	1	2	3
Universal Studios	1	2	1	2	3
White Water Rafting	1	2	1	2	3
Disneyland	1	2	1	2	3
Catalina Island	1	2	1	2	3

	Question 1		Question 2		
	Aware offered?		How likely would you be to purchase?		
Special Events	**Was aware**	**Was not aware**	**Very**	**Not very**	**Not sure**
Company Picnic	1	2	1	2	3
Kids Christmas Party	1	2	1	2	3
Bingo	1	2	1	2	3
Spring Dance	1	2	1	2	3
Over the Line	1	2	1	2	3
Photo Contest	1	2	1	2	3
Xmas Bazaar	1	2	1	2	3
Family Fun Center	1	2	1	2	3
Golf Club	1	2	1	2	3
Softball League	1	2	1	2	3
Bowling	1	2	1	2	3
Holiday Dinner Dance	1	2	1	2	3

3. What other group trips, special events or discount tickets would you like to see the Employees' Association offer?

_____

4. Were you aware that the SDG&E Employees' Association has a blood bank account for association members and their immediate families?

1. yes
2. no

5. What would you say is the approximate average discount on tickets that SDG&E Employees' Association members receive? (Circle only one answer).

1. less than 50¢ per ticket
2. between 50¢ and 99¢ per ticket
3. Between $1.00 and $1.99 per ticket
4. Between $2.00 and $2.99 per ticket
5. $3.00 or more per ticket
6. Unknown

6. What would you say is the approximate average discount on group trips that SDG&E Employees' Association members receive? (Circle only one answer.)

1. Less than 5% discount
2. Between 5% and 10% discount
3. Between 11% and 15% discount
4. Between 16% and 20% discount
5. More than 20% discount
6. Unknown

7. Have you ever attended an SDG&E Employees' Association group trip before?

1. yes (If yes, please answer questions 8 and 9).
2. no (If no, please answer question 7a and skip to question 10).

> 7a. Why haven't you ever attended an association group trip before? (Circle all that apply).
>
> 1. Do not like group sponsored events
> 2. Do not like where the group trips go
> 3. Was not aware of the trips they offered
> 4. Other (please specify) _____

8. What were some of the things you liked about the group trip that you took with the association? _____

9. What were some of the things you *did not like* about the group trip that you took with the association? _____

10. How do you usually learn about tickets and group trips that are offered by the SDG&E Employees' Association?

1. Mail flyer sent to home
2. Bulletin board
3. Update
4. Friends
5. Other (Please specify) _____

11. Do you feel the SDG&E Employees' Asociation does a good job of letting you know about the trips, special events and discount tickets they offer?

1. Yes
2. No (If no, please answer question 11a).

> 11a. Why do you feel the association *has not* done a good job of letting you know about the trips, special events and discount tickets they offer? _____
>
> _____

12. If you had your choice, how would you prefer to have the association communicate with you about the discount tickets, special events and group tickets that are available?

1. Mail flyer sent to home
2. Bulletin board
3. Update
4. Other (Please specify) _____

13. Approximately how long have you been a member of the SDG&E Employees' Association? (years) _____

14. Are you married or unmarried?

1. married
2. unmarried

15. How may children under 18 are living in your household?

_____

> 15a. What are the ages of the children under 18 living in your household?

1. Under age 6
2. Ages 6 to 10
3. Ages 11 to 14
4. Ages 15 to 17

16. What is your age?

1. Under 21
2. 21 to 30
3. 31 to 40
4. 41 to 50
5. 51 to 60
6. Over 60

17. What is your sex?

1. Male
2. Female

18. As you know, the SDG&E Employees' Association currently has membership dues of $1.00 per month. The association may need to increase their monthly dues in order to meet increasing costs. What do you think would be a fair price to pay for monthly membership dues?

1. $2.00
2. $1.75
3. $1.50
4. $1.25
5. I would discontinue my membership if they raised prices.

The SDG&E Employees' Association is very interested in your comments and suggestions that might help to improve this membership organization. Please take this opportunity to make comments or suggestions that you would like.

_____

_____

_____

_____

Thank you for taking the time to complete this survey for the SDG&E Employees' Association. Remember, your answers will remain confidential.

Return to:
Consumer Research
EB 1517

Appendix B
Sample Club Bylaws and Reporting Forms

LERC Directives

Subject: Hobby Clubs Directives

Section 1-Purpose

In an effort to offer the best variety of leisure time activities to employees of Lockheed, the Lockheed Employees Recreation Club (LERC) encourages the employees, their families, and retirees to pursue their own special interests through group participation.

Hobby clubs are given assistance to organize and function under the auspices of LERC.

Section II - Name

All clubs shall be called LERC Club, not Lockheed Club. All stationery, emblems, and similar type items must be printed accordingly.

Section III - Objectives

Hobby clubs are formed and maintained in response to interest by the Lockheed employees who have a common desire to participate in a particular leisure time pursuit. By organizing and affiliating with LERC, clubs derive assistance in financing, facilities, guidance, communication, organization, legal identity and liability coverage.

Other benefits of forming a club are as follows:

1.   To better develop individual goals in their recreation pursuits by an exchange of information, ideas and skills.

2.   To assist each member through collective efforts such as material and education.

3.   To develop friendships through social and fellowship programming.

4.   For satisfaction received from belonging to a group and helping others.

Section IV - Limitations

The LERC clubs, as a non-profit organization sponsored by Lockheed are not allowed to get involved in political activities, such as petitions in the club's name, club representatives at political meetings, or financial assistance. No personal gain from club activities should be realized by an individual member.

Section V - Membership

LERC-sponsored clubs membership are open to all Lockheed employees, immediate family members, retirees and *personnel assigned to work at Lockheed (contract employees, military personnel)*. Persons who are not included in the aforementioned categories are not eligible for club membership.

Visitors are welcome at any club activity. Visitors must be recorded and reported as such. (Caution must be exercised to ensure that the same visitor(s) are not in attendance frequently.)

Section VI- Organization

Employees who wish to form a LERC-sponsored club must provide the following to the LERC Clubs Director:

1.   A roster of members
2.   A list of officers
3.   Provisional bylaws

If this information is in order, the clubs director will recommend to the LERC Council that the club be chartered as a LERC affiliated club.

If the LERC Council approves the charter, the club is expected to conform to general policies as outlined below.

Elected club officials must realize they assume a responsibility to their fellow officers, to their club members, to LERC and the Company. They must give leadership and direction to the adherence of the club bylaws and LERC policies.

All club bylaws changes must have LERC approval and not be in conflict with the LERC bylaws.

Section VII- Finance

Correct and auditable bookkeeping records must be maintained at all times with all elected officers being responsible for accountability.

Each club must submit a financial report and reconciled bank statement to the LERC each month to qualify for continued sponsorship and financial assistance. Club financial reports are compiled into the total LERC tax exemption non-profit status and are therefore subject to LERC, Company, State, and Federal audit. They must be completed accurately according to proper bookkeeping procedures, authenticated by signatures of the appropriate club officers.

Clubs accumulating over $1500 in their treasury without a specific purpose will have their allotments discontinued until funds are sufficiently depleted.

Section IX-Additional LERC Assistance

The preceding services and assistance will be in addition to other services provided by affiliation with LERC which are as follows:

1.   PL and PD insurance
2.   LERC publicity

a. Star articles
b. Bulletin boards
c. Newsletters
d. Pay check stub ads

3. Reproduction services

4. Meeting rooms

5. Occasional sports and/or audiovisual equipment for LERC activities. A receipt will be required on loan of all equipment; it will be returned immediately upon return of the loaned equipment. If damaged, appropriate assessment will be made to replace it.

6. Liaison between management and hobby clubs.

7. 16 mm sound projectors, slide projector, VHS videocassette recorder, and P.A. System are available for club activities.

8. The LERC furnishes coffee and cups, upon request, to the Hobby Clubs Director. The coffee is made by your club.

9. Each club has a mail slot in the reproduction room where incoming mail is placed for pick-up by club officers.

10. The LERC furnishes duplicate tickets for donation awards.

Section X - Property

All club equipment and funds shall be considered LERC property. In case of club disbandment, all properties and funds will revert to LERC for deposit or be placed in trust in the event that the club should reorganize. In a situation where there is a similar LERC club in another area, unused equipment may be utilized on a loan basis.

Any major procurement of club equipment must be requested in writing and approved by the hobby club directors. Any sale of major equipment must have the LERC Board of Director's final approval. Strict accountability will be required for all property.

Section XI - General Policies

No club shall obligate itself or the LERC to term payment or contracts without first obtaining written approval from the LERC.

Publicity in local papers, magazine publications or spot radio and TV announcements must be approved by Hobby Clubs Director prior to submittal.

Clubs or members active as club representatives shall act in accordance with the Articles of Incorporation and Bylaws of LERC as amended.

Each club shall submit monthly activity and financial reports to the Hobby Clubs Director.

Each club will furnish a list of current club officers to the club's director including department, plant, building, extension, and home phone.

Keys to the LERC building may be issued to club officers having special rooms in the LERC building. When officers change, the keys must be returned to CALAC Locksmith for re-issue. Abuse of this rule may result in the loss of the keys.

The LERC building is open from 8:00 a.m. - 10:00 p.m. Monday through Thursday, and from 8:00 a.m. - 5:00 p.m. on Fridays. Any meetings other than those regularly scheduled must be requested through the Hobby Clubs Director.

Children must be kept in the meeting room and not allowed to roam the building or park.

Section XII - Review

These club policies may be reviewed periodically and any changes must be approved by the LERC Board of Directors.
Approved LERC Board of Directors, June 6, 1985.

Club Assets

Club name ————————————————————————
Date form was completed ————————————————————

Type of equipment (brief description)	LERC Tag #	Where the equipment is presently stored

Name of individual completing this form:

Club Officers Roster

Date Submitted

_____

Club Name _____

President (name) _____

Dept. _____ Bldg. _____ Plt. _____ Work Ext. _____

Home address _____ City _____ Zip _____

Home Phone # _____ Employee/retiree #_____

Vice-President (name) _____

Dept. _____ Bldg. _____ Plt. _____ Work Ext. _____

Home address _____ City _____ Zip _____

Home Phone # _____ Employee/retiree #_____

Treasurer (name) _____

Dept. _____ Bldg. _____ Plt. _____ Work Ext. _____

Home address _____ City _____ Zip _____

Home Phone #_____ Employee/retiree #_____

Secretary (name) _____

Dept. _____ Bldg. _____ Plt. _____ Work Ext. _____

Home address _____ City _____ Zip _____

Home Phone #_____ Employee/retiree #_____

Club Officers Roster (continued)

Annual club dues: $
Monthly meeting night:
Time of meeting:
Month of club elections:

•Any changes should be submitted on a new form to the
LERC Hobby Clubs Director.

•Please complete the following club information and give to
the LERC Hobby Clubs Director as soon as possible.

Monthly Activity Report
Lockheed Employees' Recreation Club

Club name _____

Month   _____

Membership of club:

      Lockheed employees _____

      Lockheed retirees   _____

      Family members   _____

      Total   _____

Attendance:	Members	Guests	Total
Regular monthly meetings	_____	_____	_____
2nd meeting	_____	_____	_____
3rd meeting	_____	_____	_____
4th meeting:	_____	_____	_____
Field trips:	_____	_____	_____
Shop/range hours	_____	_____	_____
Special events	_____	_____	_____
Other	_____	_____	_____

Did your club publish a newsletter this month?
Yes   No

Submitted by: _____
Title: _____
Dept. _____ Plnt _____ Bldg. _____ Phone _____
Date submitted: _____

Club Membership Roster

Club Name ————————

Date Form Submitted ————————

Member's Name	Employee #	Home Address	Dept. #	Plt.	Bldg.	Work ext.	Home Phone #

Monthly Financial Report to
Lockheed Employee Recreation Club

Club name: _____

Treasurer's name: _____

For month ending:_____

Part A: Balancing checkbook:

Statement ending balance $ _____

Add: Funds deposited but not shown on bank statement.

Date	Amount

Total   + $ _____

Subtotal $ _____

Subtract: all checks written but not yet shown on bank statement.

Check #	Amount

Total   -$ _____

Total should agree with your checkbook acct. register $ _____
Monies in petty cash fund/or cash not yet deposited $ _____
Monies in savings account (s) $ _____
Total worth of club financially $ _____

Appendix C
Association Policy on Athletic Teams and Tournaments

LERC Directives

Subject: **Athletic Leagues and Tournaments**

Purpose: To establish policy and procedures regarding the LERC organized athletic leagues and tournaments.

General: The LERC encourages Lockheed employees and their families to pursue competitive, team-oriented athletic activities through participation in organized leagues/tournaments.

I.   Name

       A.   All LERC-sponsored leagues or teams shall be known as the LERC League. Stationery, decals, arm patches, and all other designs must include LERC (logo) in their design.

II.   Objectives

       A.   Athletic leagues are formed and maintained in response to interest by the Lockheed employees who have a common desire to participate in a particular athletic activity. By organizing and affiliating with LERC, leagues/teams derive assistance in financing, facilities, guidance, communication, organization, legal identity and liability coverage.

III.   Organization

       A.   The LERC Council President is responsible for the selection of an Athletic/Fitness Committee to oversee all league activities.

B.   The LERC Fitness and Sports Director shall have the authority to interpret and apply the athletic league directives stated in this document as well as individual league rules and regulations.

IV.   Eligibility

A.   All Lockheed employees, retirees, their spouses and legal dependents of persons actively employed by Lockheed are eligible to participate in league activities.

B.   Girl/boy friends and dependent children under 18 years of age are not eligible to participate.

C.   Employees of the Federal government assigned to work full-time (40 hours per week) in or at the company's facilities services by this club.

D.   Employees terminated or laid off are not eligible to participate the remainder of the season.

E.   Individual league bylaws shall indicate eligibility and roster size in accordance with the aforementioned guideline.

V.   League Season Schedule and Deadlines

A.   It is the responsibility of the LERC Fitness and Sports Director to establish season and individual league/ tournament schedules and deadlines.

VI.   Disputes and Conflicts Within the League

A.   The LERC Fitness and Sports Director is responsible for resolving all disputes arising within the league. Those disputes not resolved by the LERC Fitness and Sports Director shall be referred to the Athletic Committee or Area Council for arbitration.

VII.   Finance

   A.   All team and league fees must be deposited with LERC prior to the start of league or tournament play.

   B.   All league and tournament expenditures must be authorized by the LERC Fitness and Sports Director and subject to review by the Executive Director and/or Athletic/Fitness Committee.

VIII.   Sponsorships

   A.   Whenever a LERC league does not exist in a sport or area (e.g., Palmdale, Ontario, Watts), teams may be sponsored by the LERC to participate in a municipal or other recreation league. When this occurs the following restrictions shall apply:

   1.   The team seeking sponsorship will pay one-half of the league fee.

   2.   All players on the team will be Lockheed employees, or spouses if the team will participate in a mixed league.

   3.   All team rosters are to be filed with the LERC Fitness and Sports Director or Area Recreation Director or Coordinator prior to league play.

   4.   Teams forfeiting or dropping out of leagues will be responsible for paying the LERC portion of sponsorship subject to LERC Fitness and Sports Director and Athletic/Fitness Committee or Area Council review and approval.

   5.   All teams will provide their own equipment and uniforms with the exception of game balls (for softball).

6. Teams are not allowed to have outside sponsorship.

7. No team shall obligate itself or LERC to term payments or contracts without first obtaining written approval from the LERC Executive Committee and/or Area Councils.

8. Team managers and players shall act in accordance with the Articles of Incorporation and Bylaws of LERC.

IX. Assistance

A. The preceding services and assistance will be in addition to other services provided by affiliation with LERC which are as follows:

1. PL and PD Insurance
2. Perpetual Trophies
3. LERC Publicity
    a. Bulletin boards
    b. Newsletters
    c. Star articles
4. Reproduction Services
5. Conference Meeting Rooms
6. Accounting Services
7. Checking Accounts
8. Banking of Funds
9. Occasional sports equipment for Lockheed activities. An employee signature, department number and extension will be required on loan of all equipment. If damaged, appropriate assessment will be made to replace it.
10. Qualified officials

X.   Insurance

A.   LERC does not provide insurance to cover injuries resulting from competition in the league activities. Personal insurance for such injuries is the reponsibility of the individual participants. Individuals participate at their own risk.

XI.   Property

A.   Any major procurement of league tournament equipment will be by the LERC Fitness and Sports Director. All league equipment and funds shall be considered LERC property.

XII.   General Policies

A.   Specific policies and procedures governing each sport are covered in separate rules and regulations for that activity.

Approved Board of Directors
January 1986

Appendix D
Special Event Planning Guidelines

3M Club

Also see 1. Detailed Planning Guide
2. Final Event and Budget Report

Charge Code: _____
(Must be obtained from 3M Club)

Event title: _____
Event Date: _____ Tentative Time: _____
Budget: _____
Brief Description/purpose: _____

Number of people planned for event: _____
Location of event (if known): _____
Staff contact: _____
Chair: _____
Special event chairperson from board: _____
Committee/members: _____

Suggested committees:
1. Publicity   2. Food
3. Parking   4. Games/entertainment
5. Cleanup   6. Registration
7. Other i.e., facility, decorations, awards, doorprizes, etc.

All sub-committees are responsible to write a final report for the chairperson.

Volunteers: All volunteers should get in free at the event with the exception of the Holiday Boutique and the Sun Sale (i.e., rental of booth or space). If applicable a free meal at the event will be allowed. In the case of special meetings that require a lunch you may use the budget money if the budget allows it. (It is important to remember that the chairperson and his/her committee are responsible to stay within the allotted budget).

Interim report: Minutes should be written at each committee meeting and maintained in a chairperson's file.

Note: Some events may require more or less than the suggested committees, as these are just guidelines. Every event however, must have a budget report and final report that is turned in to the 3M Club Staff contact and Special Events Chairperson from the Board of Directors. This is the responsibility of the Chairperson.

Detailed Planning Guide

Budget: _____

Event Name: _____

Staff Contact: _____

Chair: _____

Suggested Committees:

1. Publicity

    a. Flyers/registration form must be approved by 3M Club staff. The price of the event is based on the budget and is usually pre-determined by the 3M Club Board of Directors. Allow 6-8 weeks prior to the event for mailings. 3M Club Staff will coordinate all publicity in the Stemwinder.

    b. Registration the day of event—is there a limit? Is it by drawing or first come first served? Maintain a master list from the registration for check in. Are all materials needed for distribution available at the check-in (i.e., bags, tickets, etc.)? How many volunteers are needed at the registration table on the day of the event?

    c. Outside advertising- if applicable, (i.e., Boutique, Sun Sale) where the event has a public attendance, you can contact local newspapers, TV, and radio for free or paid ads if the budget allows.

    d. Posters/ banners, videos, etc.- We suggest that you use outside vendors if purchasing large posters. See 3M Club Staff for approved vendors. Note* If you want to use a logo for your event please use the 3M Club logo not the corporate logo. There is a difference! A "3M Club Sponsored event" banner is available for your use and should be used at all events. See your staff contact.

2. **Food**

    a. Will it be served?

    b. Catered vs. volunteers- compare costs

    c. Kinds of food-menu selection

    d. Facility - can food be brought in?

    e. Alcohol- must abide by the 3M Club Drug and Alcohol Policy (45 minutes).

    f. Be aware that you can use Activity Clubs to serve or provide food as they are always looking for fund raising events. Contact your 3M Club Staff for assistance.

    g. 3M Club Staff has a list of approved vendors.

3.   **Parking**

    a. If applicable, is it adequate?

    b. Is there any overflow available?

    c. Are attendants needed?

    d. Can consider off-duty policemen?

4.   **Games/entertainment**

    a. Adult vs. children

    b. Selection and quantity

    c. Checks vs purchase orders, Please contact the 3M Club at 733-6220 with the required information in regard to items needed on a purchase order. Please have the following information available when you call:

        1.   your name and address

        2.   your phone number

        3.   name and address of vendor (seller)

        4.   today's date

        5.   invoice payment terms

        6.   charge code (obtained from 3M Club) and event name

        7.   quantity, unit, description, and price of item(s) purchased (complete as appropriate)

    d. 3M Club Staff has suggested catalogs from various vendors and music groups if applicable.

    e. Arrange for volunteers if you plan on a Santa or Easter Bunny, etc.

Note

If a contact is involved (i.e., a music group, entertainment, food vendors, etc.) the 3M Club staff must approve it before implementation because of legal requirements.

5. **Clean up**

    a. Work in conjunction with the facility management.
    b. Leave a good impression!

6. **Registration** - See publicity

7. **Other**

    a. Facility
       1. Size
       2. Location - Tartan Park Clubhouse maximum capacity is 250 people. Picnic pavilions seat 300-350 under the roof.
       3. Cost/contracts (see note about contracts under games)
       4. Parking
       5. Availability

    b. Decorations
       1. What type is applicable?
       2. Flowers, i.e., what colors?
       3. Check with former committee or 3M Club Staff to see if any decorations exist from prior events.
       4. Cost

    c. Door prizes
       1. Is budget money available?
       2. If soliciting for doorprizes please project a professional image when dealing with any customer, vendor, or 3M Division. (Thank you notes would be most appropriate.)

   d. Awards/trophies
- 1.   Is money available?
- 2.   Type - i.e., trophy, t-shirt, ribbon, etc.
- 3.   3M Club staff has available vendor contact if applicable.

Chairman's final report

Attach all committee reports and a budget report.

Recommendations (i.e., changes, additions)

1. Did the event fill?

The Chairman's final report should be turned in to the 3M Club Staff no later than one month following date of event. A copy should be sent to the Special Events Chairperson - Board of Directors and the 3M Club offices.

Appendix E
Retiree Health Information Questionnaire

Rockwell Employees' Recreation Center
Anaheim

All retirees participating in the Rockwell Employees' Recreation Center Retirees' Exercise Class must complete a Health Information Questionnaire (HIQ) prior to participating in the class. The HIQ must be signed by your personal physician.

After a physician has approved your exercise capability, return the signed HIQ form to a member of the Recreation Center Staff.

Your health and safety is important to the Recreation Center Staff. We care about you.

Rockwell Employees' Recreation Center
Health Information Questionnaire

Please answer all of the following questions:

In the past 6 months have you had?

	Yes	No
Chronic cough	___	___
Chronic joint pain	___	___
Chronic muscle pain	___	___
Foot problems	___	___
Frequent muscle cramps	___	___
Hernia	___	___
Persistent infections	___	___
Phlebitis	___	___
Prostate disorder	___	___
Swollen ankles	___	___
Ulcers	___	___
Other	___	___

In the past 5 years have you had?

	Yes	No
Arthritis	___	___
Asthma	___	___
Disc problems	___	___
Severe anemia	___	___
Emphysema	___	___
Fainting spells	___	___
Heart palpitations	___	___
Kidney disease	___	___
Obesity	___	___
Respiratory infections	___	___
Unexplained fatigue	___	___

In your lifetime have you had?

	Yes	No
Angina	____	____
Blackouts	____	____
Cancer	____	____
Chest pain	____	____
Epilepsy	____	____
Heart Disease	____	____
High blood pressure	____	____
Metabolic disease (e.g.) diabetes	____	____
Rheumatic fever	____	____
Seizures/convulsions	____	____
Shortness of breath	____	____
Back problems	____	____

Participant Information

Name (Print)

_____

Last   First   (Signature)   Date

_____

Street   City   Phone

_____

Physician's name & phone #

_____

Birth date   Person and phone # to notify in emergency

Date of last physical: _____ Do you smoke?_____

Medical Release

_____

I understand I have been referred to my personal physician and cannot participate in the retirees' exercise class at the Rockwell Employees' Recreation Center until I have medical clearance from my personal physician.

_____

Signature   Date

I certify that the above person has my approval to participate in a group exercise class that is conducted at the Rockwell Employees' Recreation Center.

_____

Physician's signature   Date

Appendix F
Rockwell Employees' Recreation/Fitness Center
Program Card

Programmed By _____   Training Pulse Rate _____

Warm-up		Exercise	Reps
Metabolic:		Body Dynamics Class ———————	———————————
Stretching:			

Metabolic:
Stretching:

UPPER

MIDDLE

LOWER

Muscular Strength/ Endurance		Exercise	Lbs	Sets	Reps	Lbs	Sets	Reps
_____ Bench Press								
_____ Crossover Cables								
_____ Double Chest								
_____ Dumbbells								
_____ Lat Bar	UPPER							
_____ Bicep Mach								
_____ Tricep Mach Extension								
_____ Low Pulley								
_____ Pull-up Bar								
_____ Other								
_____ Other								
_____ Abdominal Board								
_____ Abdominal Machine								
_____ Hip Abduction/ Adduction								
_____ Low Pulley	MIDDLE							
_____ Lower Back Machine								
_____ Rotary Torso								
_____ Hip Flexor Mach (Abs)								

Muscular Strength/ Endurance		Exercise	Lbs Sets Reps	Lbs Sets Reps
_____	Other	_____	___ ___ ___	___ ___ ___
_____	Other	_____	___ ___ ___	___ ___ ___
_____	Leg Extension	_____	___ ___ ___	___ ___ ___
_____	Leg Curl Mach	_____	___ ___ ___	___ ___ ___
_____	Leg Press	_____	___ ___ ___	___ ___ ___
_____	Standing Calf Mach	_____	___ ___ ___	___ ___ ___
_____	Other	_____	___ ___ ___	___ ___ ___
_____	Other	_____	___ ___ ___	___ ___ ___

(LOWER)

Cardio Respiratory

_____	Aerobics Class		
_____	Jogging		
_____	Cycling	_____ Minutes	
_____	Other	_____ Minutes	_____ Training Pulse Rate
_____	Stair Master	_____ Minutes	

Cool down	Reps	Sec
1. Walking Two Minutes _____	_____	_____
2. _____	_____	_____
3. _____	_____	_____
4. _____	_____	_____
_____	_____	_____
_____	_____	_____
_____	_____	_____
_____	_____	_____

Appendix G
Walking Program Form

Noonwalkers Survey

Please fill out this survey and return it to the Recreation Center through inter-office mail at 058/55/AA92.

Name   Extension

1.   Do you walk during your lunch break?
      Yes   No

2.   If no, would you like to walk during your lunch break?
      Yes   No

3.   If you do walk during your lunch break, how long do you walk?
                minutes

4.   What days do you walk?   M   T   W   Th   F

5.   Would you like to join the Noonwalkers club?
      Yes   No

6.   Would you like to be a walk leader? (All it takes is enthusiasm and motivation!)
      Yes   No

7.   Do you know anyone who walks at lunch time or any-time?

Name _____   ext. _____

_____

More surveys available at employee services (Canoga and DeSoto) and at the Recreation Center. Questions? Call Kamie 710-2145.

Rockwell Employee's Recreation/Fitness Center
"Walk at Work"

Week of _____   Minute Time Chart   Group Leader _____

Last Name, First Name	Phone #	Monday	Tuesday	Wednesday	Thursday	Friday	Total

Appendix H
Waiver and Accident Report Form

Assumption of Risk, Release and Hold Harmless

I confirm that I am in good health, and that I understand the nature of the program in which I am enrolling. In consideration of my acceptance into the program, I hereby assume all responsibility for any or all injuries or damages, whether personal or property, that I may have, suffer or incur, and which arises out of my participation in the program. Further, I release and hold harmless the instructor, Lockheed Aeronautical Systems Company, Lockheed Corporation, and Lockheed Employees Recreation Club, from any and all loss, cost, claim, liability, or damage that I may have, suffer, or incur and which arises out of my participation in the program.

I have read and understand and hereby sign the foregoing assumption of risk, release and hold harmless.

Signature _____ Date _____

A copy of this report must be completed within 24 hours, signed by Dept. Manager, and then forwarded to the safety department.

Name _____

Employee no. _____ Plant _____ Dept. _____
Date of injury _____ Time _____ Location _____
Occupation _____ Job code _____
Months on job _____
Seniority date _____ Shift _____
Age _____ Sex _____

Name of witness _____

Nature and extent of injury _____
Expected time lost as a result of this injury_____
Medical limits_____
Hazardous condition _____
Unsafe act_____

Personal protective equipment required _____
Worn?   Yes _____ No _____

Date of last safety discussion _____

Corrective action to prevent recurrence_____

Describe in detail how accident occurred_____
_____
_____
_____
_____
_____
_____

by _____ Ext. _____ by _____ Ext. _____
Dept. Supervisor   Dept. Manager

Signature _____ Date _____
Signature _____ Date _____

Appendix I
LERC Programmer's Check List

Program _____

Program Date _____

Account # _____

Budget _____

Programmer _____

Pre-event		Objectives
	Check when	_____
Deadlines:	**completed**	_____
Reservations due: _____	_____	_____
Issue flyers by: _____	_____	_____
Program deadline: _____	_____	_____

Marketing:		
Flyer	_____	_____
Star	_____	_____
Paycheck Stub	_____	_____
Electronic Boards	_____	_____
News Journal	_____	_____
PE Guide	_____	_____
Banner	_____	_____
PA Announcements	_____	_____
Other	_____	

Miscellaneous:		Support (Staff, Voluunteers,
Contracts	_____	Council)
Checks	_____	_____
Prize Funds	_____	_____
Trophies/Ribbons	_____	_____
Facility Reservations	_____	_____
Camera/film	_____	_____
Security	_____	
Liability-Coverage	_____	Number of Participants
Documentation	_____	expected
Schedule Meetings	_____	_____
Volunteers	_____	_____
Contracted help	_____	_____
Rosters	_____	_____
Tickets	_____	_____
Communiques	_____	_____

Anticipated Reactions

Facility prep   _____   _____
    Chairs/ Tables   _____   _____
    Electrical   _____   _____
    Sports field   _____   _____
    Rope/line   _____   _____
Equipment/supplies   _____   _____
    Money box   _____   _____
    Calculator   _____   _____
    Paper   _____   _____
    Pencil/pens   _____   _____
    Costumes   _____   _____
    Sports equipment   _____   _____
    First Aid Kit   _____   _____
    Decorations   _____   _____
    Raffle tickets   _____   _____
    Squirrel cage   _____   _____
    Refreshments   _____   _____
    Fitness equipment   _____   _____
    Registration forms _____   _____

Appendix J
Final Event and Budget Report

Event ———————————————— Budget ————————

Date of Event ————————————————————————

Chair ————————————— Staff Contact ——————————

Committee Members and Addresses

Name 　　　　　　　3M Address

————————————————————————————————
————————————————————————————————
————————————————————————————————

Final Report

• Attach all committee reports along with Chairman's report •

*Note: A final net activity report is prepared by 3M Club Staff, which is
    formulated from your budget report.

Income
(i.e. registration fees)　　　　　Total Income

Expense:
　　　　Description 　　　　　costs

————————————————————————————————
————————————————————————————————
————————————————————————————————
————————————————————————————————

　　　　　　　　　　　　Total Expense ————————————
(office use only) Net Activity Expense ————————————

Note

It is 3M Club's policy that the committee stay within the alloted budget
for this event.

*Remember to keep all receipts. Receipts must be attached to this
  report.

L.E.R.C. Program Statement Profit/Loss

Date: _____

Program: _____

Date of Program: _____

Number of Participants: _____

Program Preparation:

_____
_____
_____

Person Working Program: _____

Hours Worked: _____

Total Receipts:

Total Expenses:

Date:	Vendor:	Description:	Amount:
			$_____

Income/Loss on Program: $_____
Amount Budgeted: $_____
Over (Under) Budget: $_____

Evaluation and Recommendations:

Appendix K
Instructional Class Evaluation

Exhibit A

We, at the LERC, are concerned with providing you with quality classes that meet your needs and interests. To do so, however, we need your input. Please fill out the following questionnaire and return it as soon as possible to the LERC Office, Department 90-73, LERC, A-1.

Name of Course _____

Name of Instructor _____

Dates of Course _____

Place _____ Time _____

Number of Sessions per Week _____

Please answer the following by circling the appropriate number. (1=poor, 2=fair, 3=average, 4=good, 5=excellent)

Class Sessions:

1. Classes were organized	1	2	3	4	5
2. Instructions were clear	1	2	3	4	5
3. Material was pertinent	1	2	3	4	5
4. Classes started and finished on time	1	2	3	4	5

Class Instuctor:

1. Attitude	1	2	3	4	5
2. Appearance	1	2	3	4	5
3. Enthusiasm	1	2	3	4	5
4. Knowledge	1	2	3	4	5
5. Rapport	1	2	3	4	5
6. Communication	1	2	3	4	5

Brief Answer

1. Was the course as beneficial to you as you thought when you
   enrolled?

   _____

   _____

   _____

2. Would you enroll in a more advanced session if offered?

   _____

   _____

   _____

3. Was the scheduled time for class convenient?   ___ Yes ___ No

   If No, what would be better days or time?

   _____

   _____

   _____

Palmdale LERC Aerobic Questionnaire 1986

For the past five (5) months the LERC has held aerobic classes in Palmdale. However, due to the lack of interest and participation the classes had to be cancelled. *Your* input is important so please fill out this questionnaire and send it to Donna, LERC, Bldg. 606, Plant 10.

1. Please check the appropriate time of the class you attended.

   3:45 to 4:45 pm [ ] 4:30 to 5:30 pm [ ] 4.45 to 5:45 pm [ ]

2. How many days per week did you attend your class? Please indicate the appropriate one.

   0 [ ] 1 [ ] 2 [ ] 3 [ ]

3. Please rate the following by circling the appropriate numbers.

	Poor	Fair	Good	Very Good	Excellent
a. Instructor	1	2	3	4	5
b. Routines	1	2	3	4	5
c. Music	1	2	3	4	5
d. Facility	1	2	3	4	5
e. Hours	1	2	3	4	5
f. Days	1	2	3	4	5

4. Did the class meet your needs?

   Yes [ ] No [ ]

If not, why?

_____
_____
_____

5. Please give the reasons why you think the classes were not successful.

_____
_____
_____

6. Please write any additional comments and/or suggestions here.

_____
_____
_____

Thank you for your time

1985 Tennis League Questionnaire

We, at the LERC, are concerned with providing you with quality tennis programs that meet your needs and interests To do so, however, we need your input. Please fill out the following questionnaire and return it as soon as possible to Donna Plummer, Department 90-14, LERC, All via pony mail.

1. The following is a scale that ranges from very satisfied to very dissatisfied. Please check mark the appropriate answer for each statement below. (VS= Very Satisfied, S=Satisfied, A=Adequate, DS=Dissatisfied, VDS=Very Dissatisfied)

	VS	S	A	DS	VDS
a. Present tennis court conditions	___	__	___	___	___
b. Level of competition	___	__	___	___	___
c. Program supervision	___	__	___	___	___
d. LERC information dissemination	___	__	___	___	___

2. Is 5:oo p.m. a convenient time to play

   Yes _____   No _____

   If it is not, what time is more appropriate?

3. Would you prefer to play

   _____ More

   _____ Less   number of matches.

   _____ Same

4. Which evenings do you prefer to play on? (You may check more than one.)

   Mon _____ Tues. _____ Wed. _____ Thurs. _____   Fri. _____

5. Have restrooms been available to you at L.A. Valley College?

   Yes _____   No _____

6. Please check mark the type of matches you would like to play in (Each category would be divided into advanced, intermediate and beginning.)

_____ Men's Singles   _____ Men's Doubles
_____ Women's Singles   _____ Women's Doubles
                                        _____ Mixed Doubles

7. Several players have made comments on the condition of the L.A. Valley College tennis courts. Please check mark the answer which best fits your opinion. You may check more than one.

_____ Courts are excellent

_____ Courts are adequate

_____ I do not mind playing on the courts

_____ Courts are inadequate

_____ Courts are in very poor shape

_____ I would rather play elsewhere

_____ It does not matter to me

8. Please check mark the court arrangement that you would prefer.

_____ Current reservations made by the LERC at L.A. Valley College

_____ Reservations made by the LERC at a different location

_____ Make your own court arrangements with opponent

9. Would you be willing to pay more for fees to cover increased reservation costs at a different location?

          Yes _____   No _____

If yes, what do you think a reasonable fee would be?

_____ For Singles

_____ For Doubles

10. How far would you be willing to travel to play a tennis match?

_____ 1-5 miles   _____ 11-15 miles

_____ 6-10 miles   _____ other

11. How many years have you played tennis?   _____ Years

12. Please check mark the level of tennis that you play.

_____ Beginner   _____ Intermediate   _____ Advanced

Please write any comments that you may have to help us develop the best tennis program for you.

_____

_____

_____

Thank you for your time and cooperation!!!

1986 Golf Lesson Questionnaire

The LERC staff would like to thank you for participating in our 1986 golf lesson program. We hope that it was a rewarding experience. To help ensure that our programs meet the needs of the participants we occasionally ask them to complete a questionnaire. Your input is very important to us. Please fill this out and mail it to Donna, LERC, Bldg. 606, plt 10 as soon as possible. Thank you!!

1. What day and time of the week did you take your lessons?

_____ Tuesday _____ Wednesday _____ Saturday _____ Sunday

_____ am/pm

2. What day and time of the week would you prefer to take lessons?

___ Mon ___ Tues ___ Wed ___ Thurs ___ Fri ___ Sat ___ Sun

_____ am/pm

3. Please rate the following by circling the appropriate answer (VS=Very Satisfied, S=Satisfied, N=Neutral, DS=Dissatisfied, VDS=Very Dissatisfied).

	VS	S	N	DS	VDS
a. Facility	VS	S	N	DS	VDS
b. Value of lessons	VS	S	N	DS	VDS
c. Instructor	VS	S	N	DS	VDS
d. Instructor's organization	VS	S	N	DS	VDS
e. LERC staff support	VS	S	N	DS	VDS
f. Other _____	VS	S	N	DS	VDS

4. Please comment on any item in question #3 that you feel strongly about.

_____
_____
_____
_____
_____
_____

5. Approximately what level of golf do you play?

_____ Beginning _____ Intermediate _____ Advanced

6. Were the lessons suited to your abilities?

_____ Yes, they were

_____ No, they were too elementary

_____ No, they were too advanced

7. Would you be interested in more advanced classes (i.e., beginning, intermediate, advanced)?

_____ Yes   _____ No

8. Were there areas which you felt should have been covered in a lesson that were not?

_____

_____

_____

9. Please write any suggestion or comment that you may have —your input is very important to us!!!

_____

_____

_____

Thanks for your time!!!

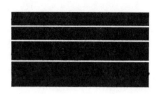

Index